BLACKSTONE'S
PREPARING FOR
POLICE DUTY

Second Edition

Phil Hardy and
Fraser Sampson

OXFORD

UNIVERSITY PRESS

Great Clarendon Street, Oxford OX2 6DP

Oxford University Press is a department of the University of Oxford.
It furthers the University's objective of excellence in research, scholarship,
and education by publishing worldwide in

Oxford New York

Auckland Cape Town Dar es Salaam Hong Kong Karachi
Kuala Lumpur Madrid Melbourne Mexico City Nairobi
New Delhi Shanghai Taipei Toronto

With offices in

Argentina Austria Brazil Chile Czech Republic France Greece
Guatemala Hungary Italy Japan Poland Portugal Singapore
South Korea Switzerland Thailand Turkey Ukraine Vietnam

Oxford is a registered trademark of Oxford University Press
in the UK and in certain other countries

Published in the United States
by Oxford University Press Inc., New York

British Library Cataloguing in Publication Data

Data available

Library of Congress Cataloging in Publication Data

Hardy, Phil,
Blackstone's preparing for police duty / Phil Hardy and Fraser Sampson.—2nd ed.
p. cm.
Rev. ed. of: Blackstone's preparing for police duty / Fraser Sampson. 2003.
Includes bibliographical refereces and index. ISBN 978–0–19–929806–8 (pbk. : alk. paper)
1.   Police recruits—England—Handbooks, manuals, etc.   2.   Police recruits—Wales—
Handbooks, manuals, etc.   3. Police training—England.   4.   Police training—Wales.
5. Police—England.   6.   Police—Wales.   I. Sampson, Fraser.   II. Sampson, Fraser. Blackstone's
preparing for police duty III. Title.
HV8196.A2S35 2007 363.220942–dc22
2006038818

Typeset by Laserwords Private Limited, Chennai, India
Printed in Great Britain
on acid-free paper by
Ashford Colour Press Limited, Gosport, Hampshire

ISBN 978–0–19–929806–8

10 9 8 7 6 5 4 3 2 1

Foreword: Preparing for Duty

Twenty-five years ago, as a young constable, I was commissioned by my first police force, Hampshire Constabulary, to write a 'Manual of Guidance for the Beat Officer'. Entitled 'Beatcraft', the slim blue book was intended to help a very young workforce meet some of the challenges of policing and to supplement their training.

Twenty-five years on the slim blue book would need to work a great deal harder, because 'Preparing for Duty' in the 21st century requires a great deal more. In that quarter of a century the police service has worked hard to professionalise, has embarked on a massive transformation of its workforce and now faces challenges ranging from Neighbourhood Policing to tackling counter-terrorism that are on a different scale. The public also expect more and, in turn, the police service expects more from the police staff, police officers, special constables and volunteers who now make up its front line.

This book meets the 'Beatcraft' challenge for the 21st century and will, I am sure, prove an important resource for all those seeking to join policing, for those new to the Service and for many inside the Service. It is also a valuable insight for anyone wanting to understand policing as a partner or a citizen. This is as good a description of the modern police service in the UK, its aspirations and challenges as you will find.

Peter Neyroud QPM
Chief Constable and Chief Executive
National Policing Improvement Agency

Acknowledgement

No book like this is ever truly the work of one person; therefore I must record my thanks to those without whom it could not have been written; to Debs and the Team for their support and everything they taught me in the years we served together and to the many serving officers who generously gave of their time to provide quotes and examples. Special thanks must go to Ray Girling, not only for the wise advice and guidance, and the many laughs, when we were Inspectors together, but also for his patient reading and correction of the manuscript through its many versions. To them and to all the people I met along the way in thirty years of exciting, frustrating, challenging and rewarding coppering I am deeply grateful.

Phil Hardy

Contents

CONTENTS

Detailed Contents

INTRODUCTION

Policing is a complicated business—and it is getting more complicated all the time. Over the past ten years, policing within England and Wales has changed dramatically and will change even further over the next decade.

Imagine for a moment that you are a visitor to London. You see two uniformed officers on the street speaking to a member of the public. Nothing unusual or complicated in that. You might assume that the officers were constables in the Metropolitan Police Service, the largest police force in Great Britain and the one responsible for policing most of London. However, they might equally be constables in the City of London Police, responsible for policing the 'square mile', or they could be from the British Transport Police, a national force that police the entire railway network, including the London Underground. All these are 'regular' police officers. Alternatively, the officers might be constables in the Royal Parks Police, or they might be special constables in any of the above forces. Recent changes in policing mean that one or both of the officers might not be constables at all but Community Support Officers, or specially accredited security staff.

In addition to the two officers in the scenario above, there will be a great many other people who, though unseen, are playing a vital part in the interaction that is taking place on the streets of London: communications staff and computer operators at the other end of the officers' radios for instance. Putting an effective officer on the street requires a large network of other professionals such as personnel and administrative staff, supervisors and managers, mechanics and technicians, investigators, scene examiners—the list goes on and on. Each of these roles and the infrastructure that surrounds them is critical to effective policing operations in any area.

Policing in this broader sense has become so complex that understanding how it all works is a challenge in itself. At the same time policing can have such an impact on our lives that it has become one of the key elements determining quality of life within a regional, community or even a family setting.

Those who take part in policing at any level are therefore entrusted with playing a significant role in the lives of others, and are presented with an unparalleled challenge. Preparing for those roles and challenges demands a lot. There is no such thing as an easy policing job. As well as the key motivational factors, physical attributes and potential for development, effective, efficient and professional policing requires effective, efficient and professional training. While much of that training will be designed and delivered in a variety of ways using many different media, there are some fundamental issues behind police duties that can be addressed at a very early stage in a book such as this.

So if you are considering a career in the police, or have been through the recruit assessment process or are undergoing training in a support or auxiliary role, this book is intended to help you.

The book is presented in four parts and, whilst it is designed to be read as a whole, each part can stand alone.

Part I starts with the fundamental issue of the office of constable. It then goes on to consider how and why the police service is organised as it is, and, briefly, considers the direction that it is travelling as it strives to provide a modern and effective Service fit for the challenges of the 21st century.

Then in Part II the role of the individual constable becomes the focus. What the job entails and what it is really like to do it are explored in some depth.

Part III is entitled Recruiting and Training. As the name suggests, what people can expect in the selection process and the training they will receive are looked at and some help is given to develop skills that will increase the chances of success in both.

The book concludes with a study of essential principles of law and then the key police powers of arrest and stop and search are explained together with the basic principles of the most common offences a street-duty officer will encounter.

There are limits on the depth and breadth that can be covered in a book of this nature, but the content has been designed to show what policing is really like for the street-duty officer and to unravel some of the mysteries of preparing for police duty.

PART I

THE POLICE

1

IN THE OFFICE OF CONSTABLE

I . . . of . . . do solemnly and sincerely declare and affirm that I will well and truly serve the Queen in the office of constable with fairness, integrity, diligence and impartiality, upholding fundamental human rights and according equal respect to all people; and that I will, to the best of my power, cause the peace to be kept and preserved and prevent all offences against people and property; and that while I continue to hold the said office, I will, to the best of my skill and knowledge, discharge all the duties thereof faithfully according to law.

If you become a police officer those are the words that you will stand up and say in front of a magistrate, usually in a public ceremony, and there-after your life will have changed. For that is the attestation, or, to use an old-fashioned term, the oath of office, and on taking it you move from being a member of the public to the holder of the office of constable.

1.1 The office of constable

The office of constable can be traced back as far as the 14th century and the idea of a local person taking an oath in front of a magistrate to keep the peace and enforce the law and, as a result, being given special powers over their fellow citizens, has been in continuous use since at least the 17th century, the days of the Parish Constable.

The fact that the office of constable is still in use is not some arcane relic of times gone by perpetuated for the sake of tradition; rather it is the legal source of every police officer's powers and the duties and responsibilities that go hand in hand with those powers. Every police officer in the country from the newest recruit through to the Chief Constables that head the individual police forces in England and Wales are constables, first and foremost.

As a constable you are not an employee. The force you join will pay you and direct your work, but it is not because you work for your force that you will have the, limited, powers to stop, search, arrest and so forth. It is because you hold the office of constable, and when you exercise those powers you are personally responsible for the actions you take and the way you take them.

You will not have a contract of employment (unless you join a 'special police force' such as the British Transport Police, Ministry of Defence Police or the Civil Nuclear Constabulary) and parts of employment law, mostly relating to unfair dismissal and contractual issues, will not apply to you. Your life, on duty and off, will instead be governed by Police Regulations and the Code of Conduct. We will look at these in detail later, but it is worth exploring their effect a little here.

1.2 The effect on your private life

If you are going to be a police officer your integrity, honesty and impartiality must be beyond question. To this end Police Regulations impose certain restrictions on what officers can do in their private lives as well as when they are at work. For example, you will have to get permission to live at any address, you will not be able to belong to certain organisations, you are unlikely, though you may if there is no suggestion of a conflict of interest, to be able to have an outside business interest, and you most certainly will not be able to actively take part in politics (though you will still be able to vote). These are some of the explicit restrictions that you will have to live with, but probably the bigger impact is the implicit restrictions that come with 'The Job'.

Once you are a police officer people will look at you differently. Your neighbours, acquaintances, people in the local pub, even friends and, perhaps, family will know what you do for a living and look at how you live your life accordingly. They will expect certain things of you.

EXAMPLE

I live in a village and a while ago I was on leave and went into the local pub for a drink with a friend. There must have been 18 or 20 people in there enjoying a lunchtime drink and meal. Suddenly, an elderly lady made a horrible rattling noise in her throat and collapsed unconscious and un-breathing onto the floor. Everyone looked at me. They all knew what I did for a living. They expected me to know the right thing to do and to do it. There was no option of me standing back and waiting for an ambulance.

Inspector (29 years' service) in a county force

When there is a problem, a collapse, a car crash, a disturbance, a serious crime, a major disaster, when all the public are moving away from the scene, as a police officer you are the one that is heading in the other direction. You are the one that is going to deal with it. It is what the public expect, it is what you get paid for, it is 'The Job'; and you'll notice that nothing in the attestation says that what you have sworn to do applies only while you are at work.

1.3 Respect and accountability

Let us just look at the attestation again for a moment. 'Fairness, integrity, diligence and impartiality', no problems there, it is what you would expect. How about 'According equal respect to all people'? Treating decent, honest, law-abiding people with respect, is that a problem?

But it says 'All people'. That includes the person you have just arrested for raping a child. That includes the violent drunk who, after assaulting you, adds insult to injury by being sick down the front of your uniform. That includes the woman who, after the fourth time you have arrested her husband for beating her up, once again says she does not wish to support a prosecution. Treating everybody with equal respect, and not just the respect you may think they deserve, is not easy, but it is what you have to do once you hold the office of constable.

As a constable you will have powers above those granted to your fellow citizens. It's true that some other people are given specific legal powers to enable them to do their work—customs officers, prison and detention staff for example; and it is also true that members of the public have certain powers to arrest and prevent crime (see Chapter 14). However, the powers you will have are far wider than those given to any other group. They include the power to:

- arrest
- stop people and vehicles
- enter premises
- search people, buildings and vehicles
- seize property
- issue fixed penalty fine notices
- cordon off streets
- control and direct traffic.

There are, of course, restrictions on when and how you may exercise these powers, and each time you do so it is on your own judgement and your own responsibility. These are wide powers indeed; powers to direct where and how people may go about their lives and, ultimately, to deprive them of their liberty. It is because you have such powers the public, which entrusted you with them, demands that you are strictly accountable for the way in which you use them.

You may have seen on television or read in the press stories about how police officers have so much paperwork to do. It has to be said that, despite the widespread introduction of information technology and anti-bureaucracy campaigns over the years, there is an awful lot of writing and administration involved in being a police officer. An incident or an arrest on the street that lasts a only a few minutes can, and often does, generate several hours worth of paperwork; though these days you'll probably be using a computer more than a pen. However, most of that work is there because of the need for complete accountability for how and why you exercised your powers. Most, if not all, police officers, of whatever rank, get frustrated by the amount of 'paperwork', but, just like having to verbally explain your actions under cross-examination in a court of law or other enquiry, it's the price that has to be paid for having the powers needed to police our modern society.

1.4 **The job**

Restrictions on private life, always being on duty, having to deal with people at their worst regardless of personal feelings and then having to be able to justify in minute detail what you did, quite aside from the more obvious elements such as risk and personal danger; why do people do 'The Job'?

Well the phrase, 'The Job', itself gives a clue. It is, in many areas of the country at least, how police officers refer to policing; indeed the in-house newspaper of the Metropolitan Police is called 'The Job'. There is great pride there, almost arrogance; it is as if policing is the only job worth doing, and for many that's true. Certainly holding the office of constable will affect your whole life and offer enormous satisfaction in a way few, if any, other jobs can.

In this chapter you have seen that every police officer holds a public office, that of constable, which is the source of the powers they exercise and the responsibilities that they have. In the rest of this part of the book we will look at how policing in England and Wales is organised, structured and managed.

FURTHER READING

→ Sir Robert Mark, *In the Office of Constable*, 1978, HarperCollins

2

HISTORY AND STRUCTURE
OF POLICING

The office of constable is an ancient one but the police service is a
much more recent institution. The purpose of this chapter is to give
you an understanding of how today's police service came to have the
structure that it does.

2.1 Policing reflects society

If you walk into any police station and talk to any of the 'old sweats'
that you will find there during a shift changeover, they will almost
certainly tell you that 'The Job' is not what it was. From listening to
them you will walk away with the impression that 10, 15 or 20 years
ago (depending on their length of service) policing was in a golden
age when villains could be nicked bang to rights and always pleaded
guilty, when paperwork was a trivial task and life was fun. Since then,
they will tell you with varying degrees of politeness, the Service has
gone to the dogs.

Actually, if you had walked into a police station 30 years ago you
would have heard exactly the same. The Service has always been going
to the dogs.

> **EXAMPLE**
>
> I joined in 1976 and my step-father, who had served for nigh on 30 years with the Metropolitan Police, did everything in his power to persuade me from doing so, 'The Job's not what it was, boy; there is too much paperwork now and you'll always be looking over your shoulder'. Well, it turned out that when he walked into his first police station in 1947 the old sweats were saying the same thing.
>
> **Inspector (29 years' service) in a county force**

Policing has always been changing; it has to because the society it is part of and serves has always been changing. The only thing that is different now is the pace of change. To see this, take a short look at how the Service came to be where it is today.

2.2 **The beginning**

The origins of modern policing date back to the late 18th century. This was a time of massive social change. The industrial revolution was in full swing and people were leaving the land in droves to seek work in the mills, mines and factories of the rapidly expanding towns and cities. Such large scale social change inevitably brought with it crime and disorder. By the 1780s it was clear that the existing system of parish constables, and the few private police forces, that then existed could not cope with the former, and the old practice of using the Army to suppress civil disorder was no longer acceptable. (The use of the Manchester Yeomanry to break up a political meeting in St Peter's Fields led to the death of 11 people with at least 400 others wounded—the Peterloo Massacre.)

After a failed attempt by William Pitt to get a bill creating a continental style gendarmerie through Parliament in 1785, Sir Robert Peel succeeded in getting the Metropolitan Police Act passed in 1829. The era of modern policing was born when the first full-time paid constables stepped onto the streets of central London in September of that year.

The Metropolitan Police was for its early years run by two men (an attempt to allay the widely held suspicion it could be an instrument of state control), Richard Mayne (a barrister) and Colonel Charles Rowan (formerly a cavalry officer). The former became most famous for his declaration of the 'Primary Object of an Efficient Police', which we will meet in Chapter 6. However, the real ethos of modern policing, and probably the reason for its acceptance and success, were the nine principles set down by Peel himself.

2.3 **Peel's Nine Principles of Policing**

Peel's Principles are so powerful and so relevant, even today nearly 180 years later, that it is worth setting them out in full:

1. To prevent crime and disorder, as an alternative to their repression by military force and by severity of legal punishment.

2. To recognise always that the power of the police to fulfil their functions and duties is dependent on public approval of their existence, actions and behaviour, and on their ability to secure and maintain public respect.

3. To recognise always that to secure and maintain the respect and approval of the public means also the securing of willing cooperation of the public in the task of securing observance of laws.

4. To recognise always that the extent to which the cooperation of the public can be secured diminishes, proportionately, the necessity of the use of physical force and compulsion for achieving police objectives.

5. To seek and to preserve public favour, not by pandering to public opinion, but by constantly demonstrating absolutely impartial service to law, in complete independence of policy, and without regard to the justice or injustices of the substance of individual laws; by ready offering of individual services and friendship to all members of the public without regard to their wealth or social standing; by ready exercise of courtesy and friendly good humour; and by ready offering of individual sacrifice in protecting and preserving life.

6. To use physical force only when the exercise of persuasion, advice and warning is found insufficient to obtain public cooperation to an extent necessary to secure observance of law or to restore order; and to use only the minimum degree of physical force which is necessary on any particular occasion for achieving a police objective.

7. To maintain at all times a relationship with the public that gives reality to the historic tradition that the police are the public and the public are the police; the police being only members of the public who are paid to give full-time attention to duties which are incumbent on every citizen, in the interests of community, welfare and existence.

8. To recognise always the need for strict adherence to police-executive functions, and to refrain from even seeming to usurp the powers of the judiciary of avenging individuals or the State, and of authoritatively judging guilt and punishing the guilty.

9. To recognise always that the test of police efficiency is the absence of crime and disorder, and not the visible evidence of police action in dealing with them.

Peel set a new model of policing, one that suited the English social and political temperament and one that still guides the Service of today.

As an aside, if ever you decide to look in detail at how policing has developed in England and Wales you might want to consider what happens to the level of public acceptance and hence cooperation with the police when these principles have been breached. There is no need to go back too far, just look at policing in the inner cities over the past 20 years.

2.4 **The new police**

In 1833, a riot at Cold Bath Fields resulted in the death of PC Culley. The inquest jury returned a verdict of justifiable homicide and were treated as heroes, but popular opinion turned when newspapers publicised the plight of PC Culley's widow. After this shaky start, the Metropolitan Police soon became an accepted, popular and successful institution.

When the social and demographic pressures of the 1840s and early 1850s unleashed another bout of disorder (though minor in comparison to the revolutions that swept continental Europe) and rising crime rates, the Town and County Police Act 1856 was passed. This Act required all counties, large towns and cities to set up their own police forces, and there were some 200 of them, following the organisational model of the Metropolitan Police. It also set up Her Majesty's Inspectorate of Constabulary to ensure forces were efficiently run, a task that it still performs, and introduced part funding of forces by central government.

The 1856 Act in effect laid the foundation stone for the unique tripartite system of police management that we have today. We will look in detail at how this operates in Chapter 3; for now it is only necessary to note the three bodies and their main respective responsibilities.

- The Home Office—responsible for policing in general, the mainten-ance of national standards and paying 51 per cent (up from 30 per cent originally) of the costs.

- Local Police Authorities—responsible for providing and maintaining an efficient and effective force for their area and paying 49 per cent of the costs (raised through local taxes).

- The Chief Constable (Commissioner in the Metropolitan and City of London forces)—responsible for the operations of their force.

The model of police organisation set up by the 1856 Act may be recognisable to us today, but it certainly wasn't the last time that social pressures have caused the police to change accordingly. The major milestones and changes can be summarised as follows.

1920s—World War I brought about the end of the deferential society where there was a ruling elite governing the masses. Though there was no increase in crime or disorder, the fundamental nature of society in England and Wales changed. Reflecting this, the Desborough Committee aimed to make policing a profession and for the first time it was possible to appoint Chief Constables from officers who had risen through the ranks.

1946—During World War II the police in England and Wales were taken under direct Home Office control and grouped into Regional Commands. In addition, central government grants became a much bigger component of the funding of local authorities. The end of the war did not see the complete reversal of measures created to cope with the national emergency. Indeed society moved to a far more centralised and activist system of government. This centralising trend was reflected in that fact that the number of police forces was reduced to 119, with far more shared services such as training, laboratory and scientific facilities funded from the centre.

1960s—A series of scandals involving senior officers plus the advent of a more mobile and prosperous society led to the Royal Commission of 1960 and the resulting Police Act 1964. This saw the number of forces reduced again and the creation of the modern police authorities. After the 1964 Act and the reorganisation of local government in the early 1970s the number of forces was reduced to the current 43. The growing problem of criminals working across force borders was also recognised at this time, and to combat it six Regional Crime Squads staffed by detectives seconded from the local forces were set up.

1980s—In the early 1980s society was rocked by a series of riots in inner city areas (primarily Brixton and Tottenham in London, Toxteth in Liverpool, Handsworth in Birmingham and St Pauls in Bristol). The full causes of these large scale disturbances were complex and are beyond the scope of this book, but one large factor was the fact that policing had become divorced from the society it existed to protect and serve (you may want to look back at Peel's Nine Principles of Policing at this point, particularly items 2 and 3). This was particularly true of the initial riot in Brixton in 1981 which followed directly on from Operation Swamp, designed to tackle the problem of street robbery and regarded by the local people as insensitive and heavy-handed. One effect of the riots was to force the Service to accept that it was now policing a multi-cultural society and needed to adapt and change accordingly, a process that continues to this day.

No discussion of changes to policing in the 1980s can be complete without mentioning the Police and Criminal Evidence Act 1984, known as PACE. A series of well publicised cases in which police powers were perceived to have been misused led to the Act, which radically reformed the way the Service carried out its business. The three big changes brought in were the introduction of national, well defined and limited powers to stop and search people (these had previously been available only to officers in some large cities); the tightening of the procedures when someone was arrested (including the universal provision of solicitors before and during interview); and the separation of investigation from prosecution (something that is only now coming to complete fruition—see section 6.2). For officers serving at the time there was a strong and almost universal feeling that the Act would see the end of effective policing, the sky was going to fall. It didn't, of course, and what was seen as revolutionary soon became the normal and natural way of doing business. It was just another example of policing having to change to keep pace with the demands of society.

1990s—Four themes that dominate the changes to the police service today have their roots in the 1990s: the continuing requirement to come to terms with a multi-cultural society; globalisation; the need to demonstrably provide best value for money; and the growth of consumer expectations. These themes are about changes in society as a whole so perhaps some explanation is needed as to how they have impacted on policing. Let us look at each in turn.

Multi-cultural society

The riots of the 1980s may have been a wake-up call to the police that they were out of step with large parts of the communities they were there to serve, but it was during the 1990s that the full impact of what that meant became clear across the whole range of public services.

For the police, the defining moment was probably the murder of Stephen Lawrence in South London in 1993. Lawrence was stabbed to death by a racist gang who have never been convicted. The actions of the police were examined in minute detail in a public enquiry chaired by Sir William Macpherson, which reported in 1999.

Macpherson left no doubt that the Service, in most cases unwittingly, provided a different level of service to different groups of people in society (what he called 'Institutional Racism'). It was from this that the doctrine (and that is not too strong a word) of Respect for Race and Diversity came, if not into being, then certainly as a core duty of the police and an attribute demanded of every person engaged in policing. We will look at what this means in practice at various places throughout the remainder of this book, but for now just remember that as a police officer you will always need to treat everyone as an individual and according to their needs.

Globalisation

All businesses, if they are going to survive, have to come to terms with the threats and opportunities of a global marketplace. For what seems to be a growing number of people, crime is their business and they are proving very adept at capitalising on the opportunities presented by the free movement of people, capital and goods that are such a feature of modern life.

In the 1960s the problem of criminals working across force borders was recognised and the Regional Crime Squads were set up to try and deal with it. In the last 10 or 15 years we have seen a very rapid increase in the activities of criminals working at national and international level. Drug smuggling and wholesale dealing, international money laundering and people smuggling have been around for decades, but the scale of these activities, to say nothing of frauds committed across national boundaries, has reached an extent that the policing arrangements settled in the 1800s have become, to use a phrase, 'unfit for purpose'.

In 1992 the National Criminal Intelligence Service (NCIS) was set up to provide intelligence to forces and the Regional Crime Squads on criminals working at national and international level. Shortly afterwards it was recognised that regions were too constrictive in dealing with this level of criminal and the National Crime Squad was formed. Both of these organisations have now been merged into the Serious Organised Crime Agency. However, the tentacles of organised crime stretch down to local level and we will look in Chapter 4 at how forces are re-organising themselves to deal with this.

Best value

For many decades policing was a non-contentious and, in the great scheme of things, a not very expensive public service. However, starting in the 1960s costs started to rise and this trend seemed to accelerate during the 1980s. The Service was not alone in this; the same held true for many other areas funded by the taxpayer. Accordingly the Local Government and Housing Act 1989 imposed a duty on local authorities generally to ensure 'best value' was obtained for the money they spent.

In 1990 the Audit Commission looked at how the police service was run and was not impressed at what it saw. Pressure was then applied for the Service to demonstrate that it was achieving best value for money. This drive has led to various initiatives and changes in the years since. One example was the setting up of the Police Information Technology Organisation (PITO), which has tried to rationalise the procurement of computer systems and so produce economies of scale as well as improving inter-force exchanges of information. (PITO is now part of the National Police Improvement Agency that we will meet in Chapter 3.)

Expenditure on policing has increased considerably in the past few years, but that trend is not going to continue and strategic managers will be coming under increasing pressure not only to trim costs but to demonstrate that they are spending their budgets to best effect.

Rising consumer expectations

At the end of the day policing is a public service, albeit a rather unusual one in that it acts against some of its customers in order to satisfy the others. As with all services, from mobile phones to health, consumers are no longer prepared to put up with what they are given by the provider.

For the police this is having a wider impact than might first be imagined. The way the Service deals with incoming telephone calls, the way it looks after witnesses to crimes, the way complaints against its members are dealt with and even the way it deals with arrested persons have all had to change in recent years to meet the demands of the public it serves. This trend is likely to continue into the foreseeable future.

2.5 Non-territorial forces

When we have looked at how the Service has developed we have considered only those police forces that are based on geographical areas, the counties and cities of England and Wales. Aside from the Serious and Organised Crime Agency, which is arguably not a police force at all, there are other forces which do an important job and deserve a mention here.

British Transport Police

The British Transport Police, affectionately known by its initials, BTP, has its origins in the early days of the railways. It now numbers around 2,300 officers and is responsible for policing the railways across the whole of the United Kingdom, including the London Underground and the Docklands Light Railway. BTP officers are recruited using the same process as in territorial forces and receive the same basic training to which they add their own specialist courses.

Ministry of Defence Police

The Ministry of Defence Police performs the same sort of investigative role as territorial forces in relation to crimes committed on the Ministry's property. However, its prime focus is providing armed security at defence sites throughout the UK. Every member of this force is trained in the use of firearms, but it also has the largest fraud investigation department of any force in the UK.

Civil Nuclear Constabulary

Formerly the UK Atomic Energy Authority Constabulary, this force was reconstituted on 1 April 2005 under an independent police authority. It has just over 600 officers and is responsible for guarding civil nuclear energy sites in the UK and ensuring the safe transit of nuclear material. Like the Ministry of Defence Police, all its members are trained in the use of firearms, and most are armed each day.

Highways Agency Traffic Officers

Though not actually a police force, and its members do not have the powers of a constable, it is worth mentioning the Highways Agency Traffic Officer patrol service. This, at the time of writing, primarily patrols the motorway network with the brief of trying to keep traffic flowing. Its members are highly trained in what they do and more recently can be found at the Department of Transport's inspection points for large goods vehicles. It is likely that in the near future the role of these officers will expand and they will be given powers to deal with traffic offences.

This chapter has been about giving you a brief, and non-political, look at how the Service has developed to reach its current status. After all, if you don't understand where you have come from it is very difficult to make sense of where you are. The key point is that there never was a golden age of policing. The Service has always been changing and always will be; it has to because it must reflect the nature and needs of the society it serves. Nonetheless, if the almost unique character of British policing is to remain then the Service must maintain the support of the public. To this end amidst all the change, Peel's Nine Principles should remain the bedrock.

In the following chapters we will look at what drives the current Service at the strategic level and then how it organises itself to meet the present and future demands.

FURTHER READING

→ <http://www.leeds.ac.uk/law/staff/lawdw/cyberpolice/pol1.htm>
This website deals with the Historical Development of Policing.

→ <http://www.leeds.ac.uk/law/teaching/law6cw/police/pol-ho1. htm>

This site looks at the relationship between the Home Office and the police. It's a fascinating read and offers a view on this very important subject not commonly aired in policing circles.

→ Clive Emsley, *The English Police: A Political and Social History*, 1996, Longman

→ Clive Emsley, *Crime and Society in England, 1750–1900*, 2004, Longman

→ Neil Walker, *Policing in a Changing Constitutional Order*, 2000, Sweet and Maxwell

3

THE TRIPARTITE STRUCTURE

Thirty years ago a police officer would go out to patrol their assigned area and deal with whatever came their way during their tour of duty. As long as they dealt with such matters as they were sent to or came across in a reasonably efficient way and were seen to be active, no one questioned how they spent their time or demanded any more of them. In recent years that has changed. Each and every officer's performance is now scrutinised in some detail and the pressure is very much on for an active contribution to their force's 'performance'. In this chapter we look at where the drive for measurable policing achievements comes from and how it affects the front-line officer.

The answer lies in the unique tripartite nature of the strategic management of police forces. In Chapter 2 we saw how this came into being; it is now necessary to look at how, after 150 years of evolution, that structure works today. It should be noted that different, but analogous, arrangements are in place for non-Home Office forces (e.g. British Transport Police and the Civil Nuclear Constabulary) and the Serious Organised Crime Agency, but these will not be considered here. Figure 3.1 shows the outline of the tripartite structure and the major responsibilities. To actually understand how the system works it is necessary to look in more detail at each of the parties.

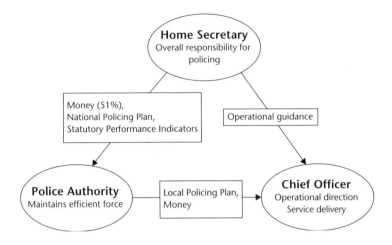

Figure 3.1 The tripartite structure

3.1 **The Home Secretary**

Since 1853 the Home Secretary has been responsible for the overall standard of policing in England and Wales and is accountable to Parliament. Despite being responsible, he or she does not have the power to direct how policing will be done. Until quite recently, this lack of power was of little consequence, as policing was seen as a non-contentious and local issue. However, from the 1960s, rising crime rates pushed the performance of the Service higher and higher up the political agenda. In addition, starting in 1990 there has been a continuous drive across the public sector to ensure that best value for the money spent on service providers is achieved. These two threads have led to a far more active profile from the Home Office than would have been dreamt of 40 years ago.

Until relatively recently the Home Office relied entirely on an annual inspection of each force by Her Majesty's Inspectorate of Constabulary (HMIC) to ensure the efficiency of policing. HMIC is made up of a small number of former chief officers together with their staff officers, who are seconded from different forces, and a small secretariat. Once regarded as a non-contentious job for retired Chief Constables, it has evolved into an extremely influential and powerful body. Its working methods have changed dramatically over the past 20 years and HMIC can now be said to have two prime functions.

Firstly, HMIC will look at how forces across England and Wales are performing in relation to specific topics. These are known as 'Thematic Inspections', and the subsequently published reports are hugely influential and have become real drivers for change within the Service. A prime example would be the inspection of police training carried out in 2000/01. The report entitled 'Training Matters' (which can be found on HMIC's website at <http://www.inspectorates.homeoffice.gov.uk/hmic>) led to the biggest change in initial police training in at least 60 years—and we will be looking at what this change will mean for you in Chapter 10.

Secondly, HMIC now looks at each force in terms of the progress they are making with specific targets and recommendations that have come from the centre. Inspections of aspects of the work of specific forces may also be carried out at the direction of the Home Secretary.

Starting in the 1980s the Home Office has tried to set objectives, priorities and targets for each force. Known at various times by various names (e.g. 'policing objectives' and 'ministerial priorities'), these were born because Home Secretaries were taking increasing flak in Parliament and in the press for the need to control rising crime rates, along with the seemingly ever-larger sums of public money being expended on the police. Put yourself in the Home Secretary's shoes—if you were taking the blame, wouldn't you want to have greater control over what was happening on the ground? From the comparatively crude objectives of the early years, the system has grown in sophistication and compulsion to what we have today.

For many years the Home Office attempted to exert influence, if not actual control, over how the individual forces worked by controlling who led them (remember Chief Constables can only be chosen from a list approved by the Home Office, and HMIC have a significant role in the appraisal of Chief Officers' performance). In addition the Home Office has for many years communicated their wishes directly to Chief Officers through what are known as 'Home Office Circulars'. These are in the shape of letters—signed, depending on their perceived importance, by very senior civil servants, Ministers of State or the Home Secretary, giving guidance as to what should be happening in each force. For example it was Home Office circular 114/1983 that pushed forces to replacing officers in back office jobs, such as communications, with staff recruited specifically for those jobs. It had to be 'guidance' rather than instruction because the Home Secretary has no power to direct how forces will operate. That said, it was almost unknown for Home Office Circulars to be ignored.

Over recent years the Home Office has developed three additional arms with which to ensure forces comply with its wishes. Firstly, there is the National Police Improvement Agency. This is a quasi-autonomous body that seeks to develop and promote best practice. This is a new agency (it will not be fully functional until April 2007), but will be come a very important one. The Home Office has stated it will:

- look ahead to identify and plan for the future challenges to face policing;
- define the police service's capacity to implement change and inform the priority and sequence of change programmes;
- find and develop evidence-based policing good practice that works, and support the Service to ensure good practice is applied;
- play a lead role in ensuring that an agreed programme of key reforms takes place;
- coordinate the future development, purchase and deployment of nationally-compatible systems and infrastructure, particularly information and communications technology;

- design, develop, deploy and quality assure nationally-compatible learning programmes;
- help the police service to recruit, train and develop its people and improve leadership at all levels;
- ensure the workforce, processes, procurement and systems that support policing are as efficient and effective as possible;
- use research and analysis and specialist systems and advice to improve policing and provide a better service to the public;
- ensure that police forces and police authorities are involved in every aspect of the agency's work.

This list of tasks was taken from the Home Office website (<http://police. homeoffice.gov.uk/police-reform/policing-improvement-agency/? version=2>) and shows just how important and powerful the Agency will be. Aside from all other matters it will have authority over police recruiting and training.

Secondly, we have the Statutory Performance Indicators (SPIs). These have come from the 'Best Value' stable and are currently the major part of the developing Policing Performance Assessment Framework. The SPIs are directed at police authorities and can best be seen as a method of measuring how efficient a force is.

Thirdly, the Home Office now sets and publishes its National Policing Plan. This lays down the operational priorities that the Home Office wants to see forces concentrate on for a three-year period. The current National Plan is for the period 2005–08 and details requirements in such issues as reducing overall crime, providing a citizen-focused service and increased partnership working.

A simple, but integrated, view of the Home Office Strategy using these three arms might be to think of as follows.

1. **National Policing Plan**—tells forces what they should be doing.
2. **Statutory Performance Indicators**—tells forces how they will be measured doing it.
3. **Police Improvement Agency**—tells forces how they should do it and helps them do so.

3.2 The police authorities

Police authorities are currently made up of nine councillors from local authorities within the force area, three local magistrates and five 'independent' members chosen from a list of volunteers approved by the Home Office. The Metropolitan Police has a slightly different arrangement; since the Greater London Authority Act 1999 its authority has twelve members appointed by the Mayor, seven members appointed by the Home Office and four local magistrates (before that Act the Home Secretary was the authority for the force).

Authorities are, then, independent of both local councils and central government. They raise 49 per cent of the money required to run their force from local authority funds, by means of a charge on the local council tax (known as the Police Precept). Their prime duty is to maintain an efficient and effective police service for their area and to hold the Chief Officer to account.

Local policing plans

The police authorities receive the National Policing Plan from the Home Office. They will then, through a system of on-going local consultation with local authorities, community groups and public meetings, work with the Chief Constable to produce the Local Policing Plan (LPP). The LPP covers what their force will do for the forthcoming year. It reflects, as it must, the national priorities and objectives set down by the Home

Secretary and how those will be met. It will also include ways to tackle issues that are a priority for the local area. For example street robbery ('mugging') may be a major issue for a force that has large urban areas, such as the West Midlands Police, but is unlikely to feature as a serious concern in a predominantly rural force such as Dyfed Powys.

The LPP will also set how the Service is paid for, the balance between central government grant and the money provided from council tax, and how the money is to be spent. For each area of service delivery that is set down the LPP will state not only what will be done, but how and — crucially — what the measure of success will be; these will include targets for all of the areas found in the Statutory Performance Indicators.

3.3 **Chief Officers**

The Chief Constables and Commissioners of the Metropolitan and City of London Police Forces are the third leg of the tripartite system of strategic police management. They are, as we have seen, appointed by the local police authority, albeit from a list of candidates approved by the Home Office, and are responsible for the delivery of policing for their force. They have operational command.

That command affords them considerable autonomy in how policing is carried out. They cannot, for example, be directed to pursue or not pursue a particular case. However, for their operational decisions they are accountable to the courts and the law, as is every officer under their command. For their management decisions they are accountable to their Police Authority. They, in practice, will need the authority's consent for major spending decisions and for how they structure their force. In particular, Chief Officers are responsible for meeting the priorities and targets of the Local Policing Plan.

3.4 **Worked examples**

To see how the system works and how it affects those in the front line of policing let's look at a couple of examples.

Domestic violence

The current National Policing Plan was published in November 2004 and covers the period April 2005 to March 2008. Under the section dealing with violent crime, paragraph 3.11 states:

> *The Home Office looks to the police service and its partners to ensure that... their contributions take full account of the Home Office/ACPO/ National Centre for Policing Excellence sponsored guidance on domestic violence.*

Then if we look at the Statutory Performance Indicators for the current year we see item 8(a) is:

> *Percentage of domestic violence incidents with a power of arrest where an arrest was made in relation to the incident.*

So the national expectation is that arrests will be made where legally possible in cases of domestic violence (the details of the guidance mentioned in the NPP need not detain us here) and that forces will be measured by the percentage of such cases where an arrest was duly made.

Now let's look at the response of a force to this. I have chosen a county force, which one is immaterial as there is probably not a lot to choose between them all on this subject. Under the heading of 'Tackling Domestic Violence' the Local Policing Plan states:

> *We have a number of clear aims for 2006/7. These include... Increase detection and conviction rates.*

The Plan also includes the following in its Key Performance Targets:

Percentage of domestic violence incidents where an arrest was made related to the incident—85 %.

So the item from the NPP has now been given a specific target by the local Police Authority. It is now down to the Chief Constable to ensure that target is met. This is attempted by the direction to the officers attending such incidents contained in the force's domestic violence policy:

Where an offence has occurred and a power of arrest is justified by the necessity criteria, it will normally be proportionate to arrest. At this early stage, the victim's views should not be sought on whether they wish the offender to be arrested or whether they are prepared to support a prosecution...

Officers are expected to differentiate between CPS Charging Standards and the law ... Domestic Violence is a priority crime, we should make full use of the powers available to us to meet and exceed targets for bringing offenders to justice ...

*To ensure compliance with the positive obligations, officers will be required to submit a report within the incident report to justify a decision **not** to arrest. This must contain all of the circumstances, including evidence sought and gathered and a statement clarifying the Human Rights status of the decision taken.*

You can now see how the chain is completed; the Home Office expects published best practice to be followed, the Police Authority sets a target figure for arrests, the Chief Officer issues an instruction and the police constables (PCs) at the sharp end will find themselves having to write a long and complicated report to justify their decision if they decide *not* to arrest.

Detected crime

In his 'Nine Principles of Policing' Peel stated, 'The test of police efficiency is the absence of crime and disorder, not the visible evidence of police action in dealing with it'. It is certainly true that reducing the incidence of crime is a key part of current policing, though it has long been recognised that the Service cannot achieve this highly desirable situation on its own. Hence, we now have for each area within each force Crime and Disorder Reduction Partnerships made up of all the agencies and community bodies who work together to reduce the opportunities and incentives for crime.

Nonetheless, a degree of crime is always going to be with us and it is up to the police to detect those offences which occur. Item 7 of the Statutory Performance Indicators relates to the percentages of crimes that are detected.

If we look at the Local Policing Plan for our example force we see that the Police Authority have set definite targets:

SPI 7a	Sanction* detection rate	28 %
SPI 7b	Burglary detection rate	18 %
SPI 7c	Violent crime detection rate	60 %
SPI 7d	Vehicle crime detection rate	10 %

* Sanction detections is a technical term relating to national
crime recording standards, and need not concern us here

It is worth noting three points here. Firstly, very many crimes are not detectable. For example in the absence of witnesses or forensic evidence it is almost impossible to prove beyond all reasonable doubt who ripped the wing mirror off a parked car during a dark night. Secondly, though they may not appear to be so to someone unused to police work, the detection targets set are challenging. If they are to be met then just about every crime that can be must be detected. Finally, the efficiency of the Force, and hence the standing of the Chief Officer, will be judged by its ability to meet these performance targets.

Therefore, the pressure is on. The Chief Officer will be looking to the BCU Commanders to deliver. They will be putting pressure on to their

Chief Inspectors and so on down the line until the buck stops with the officers who actually investigate—the PCs on street duty.

Forces now use a national protocol of best practice when investigating crime known as 'Quality Focused Investigation' (QFI). When you are assigned a crime to investigate you will use the methods of QFI either to detect it or to prove to your senior officers that there is no reasonable likelihood of it being detected. What is more, almost all forces now have or are implementing computer systems that can track the number and type of detections down to individual officers. It is probable, therefore, that your performance will be monitored and compared with your peers.

3.5 **Performance culture**

Such performance monitoring will not be confined to the detection of crime but will extended to every area of police work—how many intelligence reports officers submit (and their quality), how many stops and searches they make (and the results), how many and what incidents they attend (and the outcomes).

There was a time when street-duty officers could ignore targets and objectives coming from the centre—but no longer. The drive to achieve results and demonstrate that best value for money is being attained now permeates the whole of the Service and the tools exist to ensure that everyone is playing their full part. The police service is building its performance culture.

In Chapter 2 we saw how the police service developed and in this chapter we have looked at where and how the strategic imperatives that drive the Service come from. In the next chapter we look at how forces are organised to go about delivering the needs of society.

FURTHER READING

→ <http://www.leeds.ac.uk/law/teaching/law6cw/police/pol-ho1.htm>

See previous chapter or bibliography for details.

→ <http://www.inspectorates.homeoffice.gov.uk/hmic>

This the site of Her Majesty's Inspectorate of Constabulary; another useful place to find out about future developments and the source of many reports which are driving the Service today, notably 'Training Matters'.

4

FORCE STRUCTURE AND ORGANISATION

In Chapter 2 we saw how the current 'policing landscape' came about and how we came to have the 43 territorial forces; we also looked at the role of the non-territorial forces. Now it is time to look at how the forces are organised and how they go about their business. We will concentrate on the territorial forces—the so-called Home Office forces.

4.1 The forces

The 43 territorial forces cover the various counties and regions of England and Wales. Some forces police a single county and bear its name—West Yorkshire, Cumbria and Essex are good examples. Others cover a large city and the surrounding areas or more than one county. Examples of these include West Midlands Police and Thames Valley Police. Figure 4.1 is a map showing the force boundaries.

Some forces carry the name 'Police', whilst others have 'Constabulary' (e.g. Essex Police, but Surrey Constabulary). There is no significance to this; traditionally the old city and borough forces bore the title 'Police' whereas the County Forces were known as 'Constabularies'. However, over the years through amalgamations and re-branding

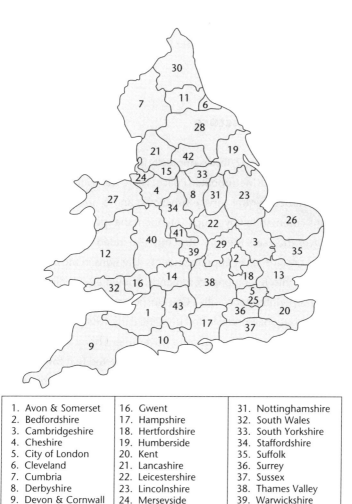

1. Avon & Somerset	16. Gwent	31. Nottinghamshire
2. Bedfordshire	17. Hampshire	32. South Wales
3. Cambridgeshire	18. Hertfordshire	33. South Yorkshire
4. Cheshire	19. Humberside	34. Staffordshire
5. City of London	20. Kent	35. Suffolk
6. Cleveland	21. Lancashire	36. Surrey
7. Cumbria	22. Leicestershire	37. Sussex
8. Derbyshire	23. Lincolnshire	38. Thames Valley
9. Devon & Cornwall	24. Merseyside	39. Warwickshire
10. Dorset	25. Metropolitan Police	40. West Mercia
11. Durham	26. Norfolk	41. West Midlands
12. Dyfed Powys	27. North Wales	42. West Yorkshire
13. Essex	28. North Yorkshire	43. Wiltshire
14. Gloucestershire	29. Northamptonshire	
15. Greater Manchester	30. Northumbria	

Figure 4.1 The Territorial Police Forces in England and Wales

Source: The Home Office

© Crown copyright material is reproduced with the permission of the Controller of HMSO and Queen's Printer for Scotland.

exercises some forces, perhaps in an attempt to appear more modern, simply changed names (e.g. Sussex Constabulary became Sussex Police in the early 1970s).

4.2 **Internal structure**

As we saw in Chapter 2, forces originally followed the original organisational model of the Metropolitan Police. There was a force headquarters, which included central service functions, and a number of territorial divisions commanded by a superintendent that policed a geographical area. Over the years the rank structure expanded and divisional commanders became Chief Superintendents. Divisions in most forces were subdivided into operational commands, known as sub-divisions, each run by a superintendent, with a Chief Inspector as second in command. This organisational model lasted until the early 1990s.

In 1990 the Audit Commission, a government body set up to ensure best value for public money is achieved, suggested that the command pyramid needed to be flatter, following the management trend of the time. It recommended removing the divisional layer so that there was just a force HQ and territorial operational units answerable directly to the force commanders. Such operational commands were to be known as Basic Command Units (BCUs). Over the next few years most, if not all, forces adopted this model, though not all took on the nomenclature and continued to use the term Division.

More recently, following the introduction of Crime and Disorder Reduction Partnerships, another model is being adopted nationwide — that of Neighbourhood Policing. We will look in detail at how this works at street level in Chapter 6, so for now we only need to look at the top level effects.

The Force Headquarters will consist of the command element made up of Chief Officers (see the description of the rank structure at section 4.3 below), administration, training and finance, and those specialist units which have a force-wide responsibility. These last are almost too numerous to mention here, so we'll just consider a few.

In each force the BCUs will have their boundaries aligned to those of local authorities; each will be commanded, depending on the force, by a superintendent or chief superintendent. A BCU can be thought of as a miniature police force. It will have its own headquarters with admin and finance staff and specialist units such as CID officers to investigate hate crime, criminal intelligence officers and Scenes of Crime Officers (SOCOs).

Each BCU will be divided into smaller operational commands (called districts in some forces), also covering one or more local authorities, typically commanded by a Chief Inspector. These will be divided into neighbourhoods covering one or more council wards with a dedicated policing team, a Neighbourhood Policing Team (NPT).

Each 'district' will also have a team of uniformed officers who are free from responding to incidents, except in an emergency, but whose job it is to provide a mobile reserve that can be used, proactively, to target hotspots and active criminals as decided by the tactical tasking group (see the explanation of the National Intelligence Model at section 4.4 below). This team will run under various names depending on the force; Local Support Team (LST) and Neighbourhood Support Team (NST) seem to be the most common at the time of writing.

The number of BCUs and their units will vary from force to force and the number of districts within each BCU will likewise vary. However, a typical structure will be similar to that shown in Figure 4.2.

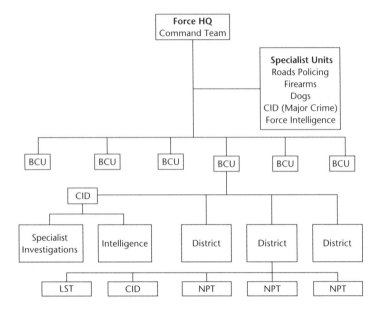

Figure 4.2 Typical force organisational structure

4.3 **The rank structure**

Whilst most officers spend most of their time working alone, policing is a team game. Each person has their role and together the effect is greater than the sum of parts. Additionally, you will attend many incidents that need the efforts of several officers to deal with them successfully and safely. Note the 'safely'; policing can be a dangerous business and as a police officer your prime duty is the safety of the public and then, and only then, the safety of your colleagues and finally yourself.

Most of the time you will be responsible for making your own decisions as to what should be done; however, when a team effort is needed then someone has to be in charge and they need to be able to give orders that will be obeyed. Very often on these occasions someone will get hurt, or even killed, if what needs to be done isn't done promptly and efficiently.

It is for this reason that the police have preserved a formal rank structure (as indeed have other emergency services such as the Fire Brigade). When the modern police was founded in 1829, society was based on a recognised hierarchy, and the pseudo-military ranks used in the police were a natural extension of it. Today we may be used to far more egalitarian ways, but when it is a matter of life and death in the next few minutes there can be no room for discussion and argument. So the rank structure is maintained.

Figure 4.3 shows the badges of rank in 41 of the 43 Home Office forces. The Metropolitan and City of London police forces have a slightly different structure above Chief Superintendent. However, as this book is aimed at those wanting to join the Service, we need not worry here about the intricacies of Commanders, Deputy Assistant Commissioners, Assistant Commissioners, Deputy Commissioners and Commissioners as opposed to Assistant Chief Constables, Deputy Chief Constables and Chief Constables. What is more important is to understand the more junior ranks.

Note the word 'junior'; in the Service there are senior officers, but no superior officers, as you would find in the military. At the moment all police officers join as probationary constables and though some may be promoted (there is the High Potential Development Scheme for those identified as having the potential to reach the highest ranks), all hold the office of constable, as we noted in Chapter 1.

The first step is to be confirmed as a constable. The term Probationer is going out of fashion, to be replaced by Student Officer. Whilst it is true that for the first two years you will undergo your basic training (we will look at what this entails later in the book), you will at the same time be a probationary constable. The word 'Probation' comes from the Latin word 'Probare' — to put to the test, and that is what 'The Job' will be doing to you. As well as passing your training you have

Figure 4.3 Badges of rank

Source: The Metropolitan Police

to prove—to your force, to your colleagues and, most importantly, to yourself—that you are good enough to be a police officer.

Once confirmed if you want to go for promotion you will first of all need to pass the national qualifying examination for sergeant. This is a multiple-choice paper on law and procedure, and requires an in-depth knowledge of both if you are going to pass it. The exam does not, in itself, get you promoted however; it is merely the joining ticket. Once you have passed the written paper then, depending on your force, you will either have to pass a nationally run assessment centre or an interview board followed by 12-month period of workplace assessment whilst performing the role of sergeant on a temporary basis. The workplace assessment is a recent innovation and, at the time of writing, has not yet been adopted nationally. Where it is not yet available, officers seeking to qualify for promotion will have to pass the nationally run assessment centre, which is strictly speaking the second part of the qualifying examination.

As a street-duty sergeant you will either be in charge of a team of constables and Police Community Support Officers (PCSOs) policing a small area, or around eight constables on a support team. Your job will primarily be to ensure that your people do what is needed and do it efficiently and effectively. In addition you will be the person in command of larger incidents requiring the effort of a small team.

The next rank is that of Inspector. Again you will need to pass the national qualifying examination (a multiple-choice examination on the relevant law) and then, as with the constable to sergeant procedure, either an assessment centre or a period of workplace assessment in the role. As an Inspector you will normally have command of around three sergeants and their teams. You will be responsible for taking the policy directions handed down from above and turning them into actions that your sergeants can get their teams to deliver, often in liaison with other agencies. You will also be expected to take operational command of incidents that need a significant number of people to deal with.

Promotion above Inspector is based on performance in your current rank and some other assessment process such as an assessment centre. There are no more formal examinations. At the level of Chief Inspector and above, whilst you will be expected to take charge of serious incidents, your primary role will be one of strategy and longer term planning rather than day-to-day police work.

Primarily because a fair number of people object to it, one thing that needs to be mentioned here is the issue of modes of address. As was noted earlier, there are times when a person in charge has to be able to give an order and know that it will be obeyed. Experience has shown that this level of action requires a certain formality in the relationship between those at different levels. Therefore, whilst on duty, Sergeants are addressed as 'Sergeant' and Inspectors and above are addressed as 'Sir' or 'Ma'am' as appropriate. In specialist departments and later on in your service these rules may be relaxed somewhat, but, for the early part of your service at least, you will have to get used to them.

4.4 **The National Intelligence Model**

The overwhelming majority of crime is local. First of all a great deal of recorded crime involves acts of vandalism and 'low-level' violence. Secondly, even so called acquisitive crime (theft and kindred offences) is generally committed by people and against people who both live and work in a relatively small area; there was study done some years ago which showed that most burglars 'worked' within a mile of their home address. Therefore, it makes sense for the majority of police effort to be based on prevention, detection and at finding solutions to underlying causes within the local community.

However, what might appear to be local crime quite often has links to a wider group of criminals. If policing is going to have any effect it must be organised to work at all levels and this is where the National Intelligence Model and the current round of police reform comes in.

For many years solving each individual crime in their caseload was the aim of each officer; and, don't be mistaken, getting detections is still a primary aim as we saw when we looked at the performance culture in Chapter 3 and as we will see again when we look at real world policing in Part II. However, some years ago it was finally realised that treating each case as single and distinct was, for the most part, inefficient. Some crimes are indeed one-offs, most murders would fall into this category, but probably the majority are part of a pattern of behaviour by one or more individuals. The principle of intelligence-led policing, where the totality of crime is considered and police actions are targeted accordingly, came to the fore in the early 1990s. Since then it has gradually been developed and refined till a few years ago the National Criminal Intelligence Service (NCIS, now subsumed into the Serious Organised Crime Agency) produced the National Intelligence Model (NIM).

The NIM recognises the need to impact at three levels.

- **Level 1**—Local issues. Usually crimes, criminals and other problems that affect at a local level, no wider than a BCU. Whilst such issues may vary from low value thefts and vandalism to very serious crimes such as murder, in themselves the crimes do not need a wider view, though they may provide information which can be turned into intelligence which, when developed, may affect a higher tier.

- **Level 2**—Cross border issues. Here we are talking about criminal behaviour by an individual or groups that affect more than one BCU or, more importantly, more than one force area.

- **Level 3**—Serious organised crime on a national or international scale, which requires identification by proactive means and a response by teams dedicated to working at this level.

To make the understanding of these levels easier a real life example may help.

EXAMPLE

Tommy is a heroin addict. To satisfy his addiction he needs considerable sums of money which he raises by burgling houses and business premises near where he lives, interspersed with a bit of shoplifting. Tommy buys his drugs from a dealer in the town centre who, in turn, gets them from a 'wholesaler' in the nearest big city. The wholesaler gets them from the importer elsewhere in the country who is part of a gang which has connections through to the Middle East.

Tommy's crimes are part of a chain which has links at many levels: at neighbourhood level (where he steals); at the BCU level (where his dealer sells)—level 1; at the regional or force level (the activities of the wholesaler)—level 2; and at national and international level (the importer)—level 3.

With these levels in mind, look again at the force structure diagram (Figure 4.2). You can see that at the BCU level there is an intelligence unit. All officers within the BCU will be contributing the information they collect during their work to this unit. There the information is analysed and fed back to inform the work of the BCU teams and where relevant it is fed up the chain to the Force Intelligence Unit, which is under the command of force HQ. Here they will be looking for and at issues which affect more than one BCU (and coordinating the response via the force command team). They will also be exchanging information with the Serious Organised Crime Agency (SOCA), who are charged with dealing with the national response to level 3 criminality.

You may have thought that forces can look after crimes and criminals who work across BCUs and that SOCA deals with national and international matters, but that there is a gap in relation to matters which affect more than one force but don't meet the criteria for level 3. If you did you were quite right.

This gap at level 2 has been in existence since the mid-1990s when the National Criminal Intelligence Service was formed primarily to gather information and disseminate intelligence about criminals working at national and international level. As an unplanned side-effect it pulled what were then the Regional Crime Squads upwards to level 3 and away from the level 2 work which, as we saw in Chapter 2, they were set up to tackle.

The problem of how to find the resources to deal with level 2 without taking them from neighbourhood policing is one of (if not the prime) drivers behind current police reform. In late 2005 and early 2006 the Home Office tried to drive through another round of force amalgamations as a way of squaring this circle. This initiative foundered on the rock of the costs involved, though, if past experience is to go by, it may well be re-floated in the future (how many forces were there in 1856?). However, political machinations aside, criminals operating across force borders are a real and ever growing problem. So you can expect to see a lot more formalised joint force squads and units in the near future.

Meanwhile it is the processes and products of the NIM that all forces are using to make decisions on the deployment of their units. Therefore they are going to directly affect you as a street-duty police officer, so it is probably worth spending a few minutes coming to terms with how they work.

We need not go into too much detail, the full scope of the NIM is way beyond this book and, not least, because every force will have a slightly different slant on how they implement the processes; but the core elements will be the same.

To understand the basics, think of the management of policing as having three parts: the inputs which give what needs to be done; what you do with those inputs to enable you to make sensible decisions that will enable you to meet the desired outcomes whilst making best use of your precious resources (which are always going to be fewer than you need); and the outputs—what happens as a result of your decisions.

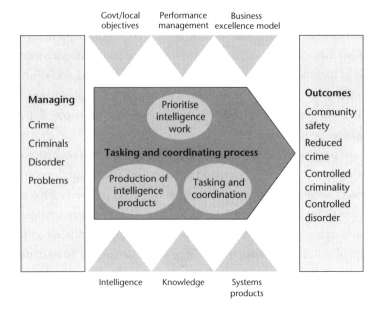

Figure 4.4 The National Intelligence Model

Source: Cambridgeshire Constabulary

Figure 4.4 gives a high-level view of how these factors interrelate using the NIM.

The inputs are the crimes and incidents reported by the public, the information that comes from community partners and, of course, there are the objectives set down in the Local Policing Plan that we met in Chapter 3. Some of the incidents and crimes will, of course, require an urgent response and officers will need to be dispatched immediately to deal with them. The information about that incident (including that which the officers gather at the scene or from their follow-up enquiries) is still fed into the system.

All the information about what is going on in the area is fed into the intelligence unit where, in conjunction with other sources (e.g. intelligence reports from officers and other agencies) it is analysed and one or more intelligence products are produced. These products vary depending on the need, level and information available, and this is not the place to go into detail. Suffice it to say that the products give an assessment as to what is likely to happen and/or who should be targeted. These go forward to the Tactical Tasking and Co-ordinating Group (TTCG).

The TTCG will meet at regular and frequent intervals and will consist of the operational commanders and heads of specialist units for the level. So at BCU level the TTCG would consist of the operational commander, district commanders, heads of local CID units together with local commanders of HQ units (e.g. the local Dog Unit sergeant). They will consider the reports from the intelligence cell and make decisions as to how the units under their command will be tasked. They will also often give directions to the intelligence unit as to what products they would wish to be produced or problems they would like considered.

The operational units then deploy to carry out the tasks as directed by the TTCG. The results of their efforts are then fed back into the system and the whole cycle repeats.

Policing is, as you will have gathered by now, a fast changing occupation. Of all the initiatives and reforms that have been introduced over the last few years the advent of the NIM is probably one of the most far-reaching and profound in terms of its effect on the work of front-line officers, yet it is one of the least remarked upon. As and when you join the Service it will repay your effort many times over for you to take the time to gain an in-depth understanding of its processes and products.

In this chapter we have looked at how the Home Office forces are organised, the rank structure and the prime method now being used to manage their business (by the way these last two apply equally to non-Home Office forces). When taken in conjunction with the previous chapters you will now have an idea about the complexity of modern policing, but apart from a look at the office of constable we have said very little about the people involved. It is now time to rectify that omission and in the next chapter we will look at some of the roles that have to be performed if the Service is going to function.

FURTHER READING

→ <http://www.homeoffice.gov.uk>

The official Home Office website. Through it you can access the official view on just about any subject to do with policing. The section on police reform is particularly useful and interesting if you want to know where Her Majesty's Government intends to take the police service in the medium to long term.

5

THE POLICE FAMILY

By now you will have realised just how complex policing is in today's world and you will have gained some understanding of the pressures that drive the work of the forces. In this chapter we will look at the roles within the Service that must be filled if the needs of the public are to be met.

5.1 **Police officers**

As we have seen, every police officer holds the office of constable. There are about 140,000 regular officers in England and Wales and every one of them started as a probationary constable. The overwhelming majority (about 97 per cent) remain in the rank of constable throughout their service and are happy to do so. For, although they may not get promoted in rank, they can move between specialist postings and so maintain a varied and challenging career. This book isn't big enough to detail all the possible roles a police officer can undertake, so we will look at just a few of the main ones.

Street-duty

Whether on a Neighbourhood Policing Team or a Local Support Team the street-duty police officer is the backbone of the Service. The street-duty PC is the first on the scene at nearly every incident, and from the moment they achieve independent patrol (see Chapter 10 on the training regime) they are expected to deal with any eventuality. Whether dealing with a domestic dispute or a suspicious death, a burglary, street robbery or shoplifter, a pub fight or a train crash, it is usually the uniformed constable who attends first.

As any experienced officer will tell you, it's the things that are done (or not done) in the first few minutes of any incident that make or break the case. Even in major investigations such as murders and kidnappings, or major incidents such as a train crash, the actions of the first officers on the scene are critical. It is almost always the street-duty PC that is there first and who has the responsibility to make sure that the right things are done.

The street-duty PC is the closest to the public. Their very presence on the street may certainly deter crime but—just as importantly—it will make people feel safer. They will interact with the public, both the law-abiding and otherwise, more than any other officer, and the reputation of their force and the Service generally is greatly affected by their actions.

For many, if not the majority, of police officers, street-duty is why they joined the police in the first place. With all its challenges, excitements, rewards and, it has to be said, frustrations (and we'll see some of these in Chapters 6 and 7), sharp-end, front-line policing is frequently held up to be the best job—which is why so many carry on doing it for their whole career.

Tutor constables

This is probably the most demanding and important role a PC can perform. Tutor constables are responsible for the workplace learning and development of new officers. They teach, guide and mentor recruits and help them build on the classroom learning they will have received in the force training school. A good tutor will ensure that all the officers tutored by them will be confident and competent to work as a street-duty officer.

Tutors need to be highly experienced and high performing street-duty PCs and have the necessary skills to be a coach and to teach. No one ever forgets their tutor constable, and the future of any force is very much in their hands.

Road policing

Every uniformed officer will deal with road traffic offences to some extent. Simple motoring offences, such as disobeying a traffic light or having a vehicle defect, together with ensuring that drivers are correctly licensed, taxed and insured, are part of the bread and butter of street-duty policing. However, there is a great deal of traffic law that requires knowledge and training above that which can be expected of a street-duty PC and this is the realm of the specialist traffic officer.

Each force will have a specialist Roads Policing Department (formerly these were known as Traffic Divisions) with responsibility for policing major roads, investigating serious crashes and enforcing road traffic law. Officers in these departments will be trained in the law relating to Large Goods and Passenger Vehicles and in carrying out vehicle inspections. They are experts in this field. Traffic officers will also be trained to a very advanced standard of driving and alone are authorised to pursue and stop vehicles at high speeds.

Although traffic officers have traditionally had a reputation for law enforcement—they are the ones who catch the speeding driver—their real focus is saving lives and making road travel as safe as it can be. They also have a very useful role to play in the gathering of intelligence about the movements of criminals (most use a car) and in detecting crimes (very few crimes do not involve the use of a vehicle at some stage).

Criminal investigation

As we will explore in some depth in Part II, the detection of crime is the responsibility of all police officers but—as you will see—some crime is sufficiently complex, or requires such protracted enquiries, that it needs the skills of a dedicated and specially-trained investigator. This is the role of the Criminal Investigation Department (CID).

It is not easy to get a posting as a detective (the process is detailed in Chapter 12) and once in the department you will probably start in a local office investigating local crimes. However, depending on your force, you may then be able to further specialise in particular types of cases. Some forces have a dedicated fraud investigation team, or you may be able go into computer-related crime, major investigations or the Special Branch, where you will deal with matters of national security, particularly relating to terrorism. One big detective specialism that has grown, in both numbers and importance, is the gathering of criminal intelligence—particularly the handling of covert sources (previously known as informers), which is now governed by very strict and complex rules and has rightly become a specialist task on its own.

Being a detective is nothing like it is portrayed in fiction and on the television. There is an awful lot of routine and a huge amount of paperwork. Nevertheless, it does offer great satisfactions that are not commonly found elsewhere in the Service. To take a complex case from the start and gather the evidence bit-by-bit to build the case and then finally, after many difficulties and tribulations, see the offender sent down for a long term of imprisonment really does make the job worthwhile.

With the satisfactions that can be achieved and the many opportunities to specialise, a large number of officers spend the rest of their careers within CID once they have won their place in its ranks.

5.2 **Police staff**

Police officers are a highly-trained and expensive commodity. Nevertheless, despite all their powers and training, they do not have all the skills necessary for all the tasks and roles that are required in the modern police service. As a result the work of the regular officers is now supported by a growing number of police staff.

In order to make the most efficient and effective use of their sworn officers, the Service has identified roles and responsibilities that can, and probably should, be carried out by other employees. Some tasks are probably quite obvious to you, such as administration and finance roles. Communications roles, together with information technology (IT), fingerprint and crime scene examination have also had a long history of being carried out by non-police officers. However, more recently, especially since the Police Reform Act 2002, there has been an expansion of tasks which have traditionally been carried out by police officers but for which the full range of police powers are not necessary. You may want to look at some of these.

Crime and criminal analyst

The analyst's role is one of the most interesting, challenging and influential that can be carried out by a member of police staff. They are normally employed in an Intelligence Unit at BCU or force level, although in some forces they will also be employed to assist on major investigations (such as murders) and may even be attached on a semi-permanent basis to an investigation unit.

It is the job of the analyst to produce the packages and products set down in the NIM that will be considered and form the basis of the decisions of the Tactical Tasking and Co-ordinating Group (see Chapter 4). When supporting a specific investigation the analyst's prime task is to tell the Senior Investigating Officer what they don't know and what they need to find out.

If the analyst uses the wrong hypothesis or makes another error of either judgement or logic, then, at best, their work will be an annoying irrelevance to the operational commanders and, at worst, will result in wasted effort by the people deployed. For this reason, it used to be held that an analyst needed to be a police officer, as only then would they have sufficient knowledge of crime and criminals to make worthwhile judgements. However, over the years, this has been found not to be the case. There are now sufficient analysts employed at various levels in all law-enforcement agencies for it to have become a career in its own right.

Investigation officers

For some years, certain forces have employed retired officers to assist detectives and others in investigations by taking statements from witnesses. These employees no longer had police powers, but as they were only interviewing members of the public on a voluntary basis this did not matter, and, generally, this was held to be a cost effective way of improving the length of time taken to complete the evidence-gathering process. The Police Reform Act 2002 took this one stage further and allowed chief officers to recruit investigation officers who would be empowered to assist officers in the interviewing of suspects, searching premises and otherwise gathering evidence. They still do not have full police powers.

Not all forces have taken up the option of employing investigation officers but more and more are doing so—and not always from the ranks of retired police officers. Indeed, the ability to recruit people with specialist knowledge into the role has great attractions, especially when it comes to investigating fraud and computer-related crimes.

Detention officers

Detention officers are being employed in most forces to assist the Custody Sergeant to process and look after arrested persons within custody centres. Indeed, some forces have gone so far as to contract this function out to a private company.

In the near future this process is likely to gather pace as recent legal changes allow non-police officers to take over the function of custody sergeants in deciding whether to authorise a person's detention, grant bail and make other decisions relating to detention that are at present restricted to those Sergeants under the Police and Criminal Evidence Act 1984.

Police Community Support Officers

The Police Reform Act 2002 allowed chief officers to appoint Community Support Officers (PCSOs) to work in uniform on the streets to assist in providing a visible police presence and assist with tackling anti-social behaviour. PCSOs were given only limited powers, such as being able to issue certain fixed penalty tickets. They had to call for a sworn officer if they came across anything more serious. As they had much less power and responsibility than a constable they could be trained much faster and were held to be cheaper to employ. Therefore, most, if not all, forces saw the benefits of PCSOs in providing public reassurance, as well as being extra eyes and ears within the community to help with intelligence gathering and to assist with certain investigative tasks (house-to-house enquiries for example). They have been recruited in quite large numbers and have, generally, been a success.

The Government has now introduced legislation to extend the powers available to PCSOs and a great many more will be recruited during the next few years.

5.3 **Special constables**

No discussion of the police family can be complete without mentioning the role of the special constable. We saw in Chapter 1 that constables are citizens in uniform. The 'Specials' exemplify that ideal. They are sworn officers who receive comprehensive training, wear regular police uniform and—when on duty in their own or a neighbouring force area—have all the powers of regular constables. The difference is that they are volunteers who work as police officers in their spare time and for no financial reward.

Typically, Specials will patrol busy areas during times when crime and disorder is likely (town centres on Friday and Saturday evenings, for example). They are also deployed to carry out front-line duties at major events and are a valuable resource in the event of a serious and prolonged incident. Specials are also valuable because they genuinely are a part of the community they serve and so can help bridge gaps in understanding on both sides. The number of special constables has declined in recent years but their contribution has been widely recognised, so many forces are actively trying to recruit more.

In this chapter we have taken a look at some of the roles that support the work of regular police officers and go to make up the wider police family. In doing so we have concluded our examination of how the police is structured and organised. In the next part of the book we examine what the job of a police officer is and what it is like to do it.

FURTHER READING

→ <http://www.homeoffice.gov.uk>

PART II

THE JOB

6

A POLICE OFFICER'S JOB

In this chapter we take a look at what policing is about, what has to be done. In Chapter 7 we will look at what it is really like to actually be out there doing 'The Job'.

As we saw in Chapter 2, modern policing in England and Wales dates back to the founding of the Metropolitan Police on 29 September 1829. Richard Mayne, one of the joint Commissioners laid down the ethos of the new service when he wrote:

> The primary object of an efficient police is the prevention of crime: the next that of detection and punishment of offenders if crime is committed. To these ends all the efforts of police must be directed. The protection of life and property, the preservation of public tranquillity, and the absence of crime, will alone prove whether those efforts have been successful and whether the objects for which the police were appointed have been attained.

Arguably, if today's police service delivered on Mayne's primary object it would be judged to be very successful. Therefore, essentially the role of the police in England and Wales has not changed in over 170 years, since the 'New Police' was founded. However, in that time society has changed dramatically, and become far more complex and sophisticated in the process. Additionally, because policing is rooted in the society it serves, policing has likewise become far more complex and sophisticated. So let's look at what the modern Service needs to do in pursuit of the 'Primary Object' and how it goes about its work.

6.1 **Maintaining a tranquil society**

Essentially there are three tasks under this heading, keeping the peace, preventing crime and, just as importantly, reducing the fear of crime. Originally, and until quite recently, the primary method used to do all three was to have constables each patrolling a defined area on foot and dealing with whatever they came across as they walked their beat. The presence of the smartly and distinctly uniformed officer, carrying no overt weapon, provided the public with reassurance that all was well. Being on foot, the officers were approachable, and had the time to see what was happening around them and deal with it. There is no doubt that this method of policing was popular with the public, as shown by the frequent calls for more 'Bobbies on the beat' still to be heard almost daily from the press, community leaders and politicians. It was also great fun; to be out interacting with the public, dealing with their concerns and having the time to detect offences and offenders for oneself was a wonderful job. Unfortunately, the 'Bobbie on the Beat' model of policing requires a large number of officers if it is to be effective.

From the early 1960s the growth in both population and town size was not matched by a corresponding increase in police numbers. Additionally the amount of crime reported by the public rocketed during the same period (in London there were a total of 188,000 crimes reported in 1960, for 2003 the figure was 1,058,000). As well as reporting more crimes, the public demands on the Service have dramatically increased, and people have become increasingly more sophisticated in how they want their demands to be met. To satisfy these requirements, more and more officers have had to be taken from beat duty and into specialist posts, leaving insufficient numbers to provide an effective Service using the traditional model.

It could also be cogently argued that traditional beat work was not terribly efficient in either deterring or detecting crime. In a large measure this was caused by the fact that as towns got bigger and the number of officers available for foot patrol got smaller the beats got bigger and bigger. Once the point was reached when the officer was unable to get round the whole of their beat at least once in a shift the chances of their preventing a crime by their very presence or coming across a crime in progress became terribly small.

Finally, having officers patrolling at their own discretion, whilst it might be enjoyable for them, was not the best method for the force to meet its performance targets, and, as we saw in Chapter 3, measures of performance have become fundamental to the modern police service.

Taken all together, you are most unlikely to be required or, depending how you look at it, allowed to police in the traditional method of discretionary foot patrol. So if old-fashioned beat Bobbies have gone, how does the modern Service go about its task of maintaining a tranquil society?

The first thing to note is that preventing crime and keeping the peace is no longer something the police service is expected to tackle on its own. As a result of the Crime and Disorder Act 1998 every local area has a Crime and Disorder Reduction Partnership (CDRP). There are 373 of these in England and Wales and they bring together the police, police authorities, local authorities, other agencies and businesses in the area to develop and implement strategies for stopping and if necessary dealing with crime and disorderly behaviour.

The latest policing model, which, at the time of writing, looks as if it is to be adopted throughout England and Wales, involves force internal boundaries to be aligned to those of the local authority, thus creating a clear link between the policing team for an area and the CDRP. Furthermore, within those internal boundaries, beats will be aligned to one or more council wards and each beat will have a dedicated policing team. The make-up of those teams is likely to vary from force to force; some are suggesting they will have a sergeant, two constables and perhaps six Police Community Support Officers

(PCSOs—see Chapter 4); others seem to be going for a constable as a Beat Specialist and a number of PCSOs.

Whatever the make-up of the team, the key element is that it will look at crime and disorder locally not as isolated incidents but to see whether the offending and/or anti-social behaviour is part of a pattern that degrades the quality of life for all concerned—victims, neighbours and offenders. If it is part of a pattern the team will work with other agencies (e.g. housing, street lighting—whatever is needed) to come up with a solution that will at least break the pattern. Targeted patrolling by members of the team, or other officers co-opted for the purpose, may form part of the solution, as might other purely police interventions, such as the execution of search warrants. The key point here is that the policing activity is directed to some clear purpose as part of an overall plan.

An obvious example of targeted patrolling, in which you will almost certainly take part, is that relating to keeping the peace in town centres at night. Whether you work in a large city or a medium-sized town it is regrettably a sad fact of life that on Thursday, Friday and Saturday nights substantial numbers of young people will visit the pubs and clubs and get drunk. The consequent and all too frequent public disorder requires numerous police officers to be deployed mainly on foot.

The other, though far less frequent, cause for officers in uniform to be deployed in substantial numbers comes under the misleading heading of 'Public Order'. Here we are talking about large-scale public demonstrations, with or without the threat of violence. On such occasions a great deal of pre-planning takes place in order that the demonstrators may air their views peacefully, but any trouble makers are contained as quickly as possible. The role of officers deployed will vary from simply escorting the demonstration, to being part of a specially equipped and trained Police Support Unit (PSU) to be deployed in the event of serious trouble, complete with shields, riot helmets, flame-proof suits and so forth, or as a member of an Evidence Gathering Team (EGT) with a video recorder to film evidence of offences taking place.

Fortunately the times when you will be required to deploy for 'Public Order' situations will be the exception rather than the rule, and if you are not posted as a member of a beat team, or other specialist post, your job will probably be as a member of a response section. The job of 'Response' is organised differently from force to force; however, you can expect to be working in a car, answering calls from members of the public, investigating your own caseload of crimes, and generally dealing with what comes your way. Although you'll be in a car, the response section job is the nearest you are likely to come to traditional discretionary patrolling; just don't expect to have much time to detect offences and offenders for yourself.

6.2 **Investigation of crime**

Once a crime has been committed it is the job of the police to gather the evidence and put the facts (and evidence) before the Crown Prosecution Service (CPS). It is no longer the role of the police to put the offender before the court and it certainly isn't their task to become involved in the punishment of offenders, as in Mayne's 'Primary Object'.

Of course it will be your job to identify the offender and where necessary and appropriate arrest them, but the arrest should nowadays be thought of as part of the evidence-gathering process. Once you have all the evidence the representative of the CPS will, in almost all crime cases, decide what if any charges should be brought, not you or any other police officer.

Crime can be thought of as falling into four categories:

- major crime (e.g. murder);
- specialist crime (e.g. sophisticated frauds);

- priority crime (e.g. burglary of people's homes);
- volume crime (e.g. minor theft, taking cars without consent).

Major crimes are investigated by teams of detectives headed by a senior officer who has been trained and is qualified for the role of Senior Investigating Officer. Such crimes involving children or which otherwise generate a high profile and huge public interest can require teams several dozen strong. It is not likely that as a street-duty officer you will become involved in this type of investigation.

Detectives are specialists in the investigation of crime, but some crimes are so complex by their nature that they require specialist detectives to investigate them; economic crime falls into this category. Here we are thinking of sophisticated frauds involving the manipulation of money, stocks and bonds, or even whole companies. Again it is most unlikely that any street-duty officer will become involved in such cases.

Priority crimes are crimes which may be quite common, yet are sufficiently disturbing to the public that the force has decided to detect as many as possible by ensuring that they are investigated by detectives. The burglary of someone's home would be a typical example. The list of crimes in this category may differ from force to force, as will the procedures to be followed before the CID take over, but as a street-duty officer you will commonly be the first officer to attend the scene and you will be expected to start the investigation off.

Volume crimes are the most common offences and are the ones that are generally regarded as less serious—though remember the victims may have a different view. As a street-duty officer you will be expected to carry out the whole investigation from the initial report through, hopefully, to detection and final disposal. Sometimes it is clear from the outset who the offender is, and all the evidence, including the arrest of the offender, can be gathered very quickly. Sometimes it is equally obvious very quickly that there is almost no hope of ever gathering sufficient evidence to identify let alone prosecute the offender. These crimes can be filed as undetected. Most commonly, though, is the situation where, with some work, it may be possible to find the evidence to prove beyond reasonable doubt who the offender was. Such crimes as these, called in some forces 'Status 2s', remain with the investigating officer until all the work has been done and the case is either 'solved' or it becomes clear that sufficient evidence will not be forthcoming. It is common for street-duty officers to have a non-trivial number of Status 2 crimes on the go at any one time (15 to 20 is certainly not unusual) and we will come back to look at some of the problems this workload causes in Chapter 8.

We saw in Chapter 3 that the number of crimes detected form an important measure of a force's performance. Senior officers are therefore very keen that every crime that can be detected is detected. Quite rightly so, I am sure you will agree. To this end the Service is adopting the Professionalising Investigation Programme (PIP). PIP is designed to improve the quality of investigations and so ensure that more cases are detected and prosecuted successfully by the CPS. There are three levels of qualification in PIP and all street-duty officers will have to show that they are competent at Level 1 (detectives must qualify at Level 2 and Senior Investigating Officers at Level 3). In terms of investigating crime, PIP is probably the most radical and far-reaching change to hit the Service for a generation.

6.3 **General police duties**

When the Metropolitan Police was founded policing was simple; it was, as we have seen, about keeping the peace, preventing crime and, where crime was committed, catching the offenders and putting them before the courts. Since then, as successive governments have legislated to deal with new issues in an increasingly complex society, the Service has taken on more and more responsibilities.

In part the Service was given, or took on, these responsibilities simply because it is always there. Twenty-four hours a day every day of the year the police are available to the public, almost from the beginning they have been the agency of last resort for anyone with a problem. Remember too that many of the public agencies that now seem obvious candidates for some police roles simply did not exist until relatively recently. The other reason why the extra responsibilities came to the Service was that if the matters were not dealt with properly then crime and/or disorder was likely to follow, so it was in the best interest of society that the police took them on.

These sundry roles and responsibilities are known in the Service as general police duties. They are not as widespread as once they were; you won't find constables issuing permits for pigs to be moved any more, for example; but they still can take up a significant amount of time. Let's look at some of them.

Sudden death

When a person dies the death must be reported to the coroner for the area unless a medical practitioner can immediately certify the cause of death and that it was from natural causes; there are strict rules governing when such a certificate can be issued. Although coroners have their own officers to make follow-up enquiries and deal with the administration, unless the death happened in a hospital or hospice or such similar place, a police officer will have to attend the scene, and as a street-duty officer this is going to be one of your frequent tasks. Your job will be to examine the body and the scene to ensure that there are no indications that the death involved a criminal offence (if there is any such suggestion, then, of course, you will be treating it as a crime scene and the wheels for a homicide investigation will start to turn) and to speak to any relatives or witnesses to gather the initial evidence on which the coroner can base the decisions in the case.

Licensing

The sale and consumption of alcohol have, as we have seen, a strong and direct link with disorder on the streets. Since the Licensing Act 1872 the police have always had an involvement in enforcing the regulations and restrictions applied to licensed premises. Since the most recent Act came into force in 2005, the Service now takes a far more partnership-based approach with the local authority. Nevertheless you can expect to be involved with ensuring pubs and clubs are being run correctly and lawfully.

Firearms legislation

Since the early part of the 20th century the laws controlling the ownership of firearms have become ever more restrictive and it is the duty of the police to administer and enforce the legislation (as an aside, the use of firearms by criminals has increased exponentially in the same period, but that need not detain us here). Most forces now employ specialist police staff members to deal with individuals' firearms licenses, but if you work in a rural area you will inevitably become involved.

Missing persons

When a person, be it a child or an adult, goes missing it is to the police that people naturally turn, and over the years it has become established that the police have a common law duty to investigate such reports. After a number of high profile cases, there is now a national protocol as to how missing person cases are to be investigated. Whilst it is not appropriate to go into detail here, the key element is that all reports are treated from the basis that the disappearance is crime-related until the contrary can be shown. Particular attention will always be paid to missing children and vulnerable adults as they are at the most risk of being the victim of criminals. Though the national protocol suggests that an inspector is always the officer in charge of a missing person enquiry, it is usually the job of a street-duty constable to take the initial report and conduct the first enquiries.

Child protection

Protecting children from physical, sexual or emotional abuse is part of the core business of policing. Much of this work is carried out by specialist officers in liaison with local social services departments, health and educational authorities and charities such as the National Society for the Prevention of Cruelty to Children (NSPCC). However, every officer has a duty to take action when needed and all constables, when they reasonably believe a child may suffer significant harm, have powers to take children to suitable accommodation as a temporary measure.

Mental health

People with mental health difficulties tend to be amongst the most vulnerable adults in society. Some with particular conditions will often come to the notice of the police because of their behaviour in public. Only in a very small minority of cases will they present a danger to others; they are far more likely to be at risk themselves. As a street-duty officer you can expect to be the first officer to respond to such cases and you will have powers under the Mental Health Act 1983 to remove the person to a place of safety if it is necessary to do so for their own protection.

Lost and found property

There is no requirement in law for the police to deal with lost and found property. It is simply one of those duties that the Service has assumed over the years, probably because there was no other agency to take it on. Probably there are only two things worth mentioning here; always deal with property that is handed to you absolutely correctly (more officers have got into trouble over property than any other cause) and always consider whether the item of found property may actually be evidence of a crime.

6.4 **Road policing**

You may think that policing traffic on the roads is something that has come about with the advent of the motor car in the 20th century. In fact police involvement in enforcing traffic law can be traced back to at least 1861 when section 35 of the Offences Against the Person Act of that year stated:

> *Whosoever, having charge of any carriage or vehicle, shall by wanton or furious driving or racing, or other wilful misconduct, or by wilful neglect, do or cause to be done any bodily harm to any person whatsoever shall be guilty of a misdemeanour ... liable to two years imprisonment with or without hard labour.*

A similar section covered 'wanton and furious cycling' on a bicycle (both sections remain in force, by the way).

To many, traffic policing is seen as catching speeding motorists and dealing with collisions. Yet the Offences Against the Person Act pointed to the underlying ethos. It is all about preventing people from getting hurt. Whether it is enforcing speed restrictions, drink drive laws, requiring people to get their cars fixed when they contravene the regulations regarding construction and use (e.g. bald tyres), the aim is to make our roads safer.

Over the years, traffic law has expanded and become more and more complex and traffic policing has become a specialism in its own right; each force has its own Roads Policing Department, and, as we noted in Chapter 2, the Highways Agency now has its own officers enforcing some laws. Nevertheless, all front-line officers will be involved in enforcing at least some of the simpler laws and regulations (e.g. drinking and driving).

As a street-duty officer you will probably also want to bear in mind that very few crimes don't involve the use of a motor vehicle. Even if the car is not directly used in the crime, criminals may use one to go about their business and whilst they are driving they may be committing other traffic-related offences.

6.5 Intelligence

Any examination of the work of the modern police service would be incomplete without some mention of the role of criminal intelligence. Whilst arrangements for the gathering and sharing of intelligence at local and force levels have existed since the role of 'Collator' was introduced in the late 1960s, too often intelligence has been seen as something of black hole into which information was poured but nothing ever came out again, and/or something which only applied to serious and organised crime.

Although moves were made in the early to mid-1990s to move towards 'intelligence-led policing', it has only been with the formulation and adoption of the National Intelligence Model (NIM) that a coherent and useful method of working at all levels—local, force-wide and national/international—of the Service has been possible.

Some parts of the police intelligence arena are the preserve of specialists. For example, the handling of informants, which now comes under the title of Covert Human Intelligence Sources (CHIS), can only be undertaken by officers with particular training. However, intelligence is symmetrical; the quality of the output depends on the quality of the inputs. If the information going into the system is lacking then nothing useful is ever going to come out of it.

In this chapter we have looked at some of the key elements that go into modern policing. There are of course more that could have been mentioned, national security work and the tactical use of firearms to name but two. But as these are far outside the experience of most officers in their early years of service they really fall outside the scope of this book. During your training and certainly once you have achieved independent patrol status you will be expected to deal with all the tasks mentioned above. In the next chapter we will look at what that means in practice.

7

WHAT IT IS LIKE

So far you have seen how the police is organised and what it exists to do. The aim of this chapter is to give you a feel for what it is actually like to do 'The Job'. With this in mind, a number of currently serving officers were asked to contribute their thoughts and experiences, which they did, with the honesty and candour you would expect. These officers are from a number of forces and have a wide variety of service, from just a couple of months to more than 29 years, and with ranks ranging from student officer to Chief Constable. You may find their comments illuminating.

7.1 **Why do it?**

Different people join for different reasons; when asked the question 'Why did you join?' these were some of the replies that were forthcoming and they represent a fair cross section of the total:

'I wanted a profession that was varied, challenging, and different and in public service—policing has fulfilled all of those and more.'
Chief Constable of a county force

'I had completed my degree and wanted to work in a community I was familiar with, in a demanding role with close contact with the public. I was attracted by the idea of working as part of a highly trained team, and giving a quality service to the public.' **Sergeant in a county force**

'I joined the police at the age of 32 and had worked in a variety of jobs ranging from chef to selling advertising. I had reached a point in my life where I felt I needed a career and as corny as it might sound, I wanted to do something worthwhile.' **PC in a county force**

'I had just come out of the army, thought I had no useful skills for civvy street (wrongly) and could not bear the thought of going back to work in an office.' **Inspector in a county force**

'I wanted to be dealing with people, and I felt I wanted to make a difference to others.' **PC in a county force**

'I joined looking for a job which gave variety, security and a good wage. I also wanted a career doing something where I was making my own decisions.' **Sergeant in a county force**

'Like father like son! I never wanted to do anything else and remain as enthusiastic today with 28 years service as I did then.'
Detective Inspector in a county force

'I joined because I did not want a predictable job or that I would be stuck in an office all day every day. I wanted something that I would get a buzz from and would give me an incentive to go to work every day.'
Detective Sergeant in a large city force

Unpredictable, varied, challenging, making a difference—these are the words that just about any police officer will use to describe their job. If you probe a little deeper you will get to what it really is that they find so irresistible about 'The Job'.

'Dealing with the stuff we do, it just seems as I am living more intensely than "normal" people.'
PC (5 years' service) working in an inner city area

If you listen carefully when police officers are talking about their job, it is possible to pick out the specific feelings that are part of everyday police work. The most common are excitement, frustration, challenge and a sense of reward. Let us look at some examples.

7.2 **Excitement**

It would be very wrong if, after reading this book, you went away with the impression that every day is a constant round of exciting jobs—that would be far from the truth. However, there are times when the adrenaline really starts to pump.

Blues and twos

Driving a police car with the blue lights flashing and the sirens wailing will certainly get the heart going.

> *'When you are on a shout it's scary and exciting at the same time. You never know what some idiot driver is going to do in front of you but you know you have to get there—especially if one of your mates is down.'*
> **PC (3 years' service) working in an inner city area**

> *'The first time I was in a car with blue lights going it was fantastic.'*
> **PC (6 months' service) working in a large town**

> *'When I was a response vehicle driver, every time I had to drive on blues and twos I hated it. I was always scared . . . but when it was over I couldn't wait to do it again. It was like a drug.'*
> **Sergeant (17 years' service) now in a training post.**

The thrill of the chase

Not all the excitement that an officer gets is of the adrenaline-pumping, heart-pounding sort.

> 'Sometimes, when investigating a crime, something happens—a witness says something or the scientific people call and you **know** with a bit of effort you are going to win this one. You are spurred on and can't stop working. It's a great feeling.'
>
> **Detective Inspector (20 years' service) in Specialist Investigations**

> 'We set it [the trap] up and then had to wait. It was a very nervy time. Then they took the bait. Brilliant, it was brilliant.'
>
> **Inspector (29 years' service) formerly in the NCIS**

> 'I enjoy catching criminals that believe themselves to be too good to be caught.'
>
> **Acting Detective Inspector in a rural force**

As mentioned above, not every day's duty will include thrills and exhilaration. For every minute of excitement there are several hours of tedium.

7.3 Frustration

The boredom and frustration that are inherent in 'The Job' come from many causes as the next set of examples will illustrate.

Boring duties

A good officer needs to be diligent, alert and proactive, but sometimes, with the best will in the world, the duty he or she is given is just plain boring.

'Last Sunday I was on the cordon for it [an extensive search in a rural area in relation to counter terrorism]. Twelve hours stood in a field in the middle of nowhere. Bored or what?'

PC (22 years' service) currently in a training post

'What about foot patrol? Looking back, I used to enjoy it, but there were times—second half of nights in November, freezing cold, peeing down with rain and not a soul about, not fun at all.'

Sergeant (23 years' service)

A lot of the time if you are switched on and industrious you can avoid boredom, but some of the frustrations of the job just cannot be evaded.

Villains getting away with it

Sometimes, no matter how hard you try, the evidence is just not there, and, whilst you may be certain the person is guilty, you are never going to be able to prove it. This is a great source of frustration to many if not all officers.

'It was the look on his face as the custody sergeant gave him his property back that got me; that supercilious smirk.'

PC (10 years' service) working in a small town

'I was stuffed. I knew he had done it, and he knew that I knew, but I could never prove it and he knew that too.'

Detective Inspector (20 years' service) in Specialist Investigations

'When things go wrong—and they inevitably do in policing because it is a high risk occupation—people are quick to criticise and slow to remember the times when we got it right.'

Chief Constable of a county force

'...understanding that justice is rarely done, and having to carry on working hard to investigate crimes that you know aren't going to get justice for the victim.'   **PC in a county force**

Waiting for others

Every person who is arrested is entitled to have a solicitor present when they are interviewed. So when he or she exercises this right, and most prisoners do, the interview cannot start until the solicitor has arrived and consulted his client. The officer just has to wait. Additionally, if the person is a juvenile or may not fully understand what is going on (perhaps because they cannot read and write) they can only be interviewed in the presence of an independent adult. Solicitors and independent adults are often very busy and are not available when needed, but nothing can happen until they arrive.

'I seem to spend half my life hanging around custody blocks waiting for solicitors or IAs. Five hours I was [waiting] yesterday.'
PC (3 years' service) working in a medium-sized town

When first aid doesn't work

All police officers are trained in first aid, but most go through their service never having to use it to any great degree. So when you have to put your training into practice when someone's life is on the line it can be very stressful. When you do it right and it works the feeling is fantastic; when, despite your best efforts, things don't work out the frustration can be overwhelming.

'It had been a bad few weeks for me, I'd gained the unfortunate title of ''Doctor Death'', following numerous sudden death incidents which

I had attended during the shift week. Then followed the worst few days of my career, with major highs and very sad lows. It first started when I attended a double fatal road traffic crash on the outskirts of town. I was the first on the scene and still fairly young in service, but I had a good idea of what to do and got on with it.

It was the following day when my worst day happened, thinking things can't get any worse. A call came in over the air for a unit to attend sheep on the road in a nearby village. I called up ... and started the drive down the country lanes to the location of the sheep.

My route took me to a steep hill, half way up I came across two cyclists, one of whom was lying on the floor. My initial thoughts were that he had been knocked over by a car. I stopped the car and asked if I could help. I was then informed that the cyclist had collapsed going up the hill. Myself and the other cyclist immediately began first aid, and all my training was put to use. I quickly called for an ambulance once we discovered that he was having a heart attack.

CPR is hard work, as I found out. We kept him going for about 20 minutes whilst we waited for the paramedics to arrive. He was then ventilated and shocked several times and rushed to hospital.

I was really pleased with myself, having saved someone's life, especially given the previous weeks' incidents. Then the call came over the air about an hour later. The operator said 'Your man has just died in hospital'.

I sat in the car on my own for about half an hour gathering my thoughts. I'd been on such a high to such a low in a short space of time. I was devastated.'

PC (now with 9 years' service) currently in a training post

'... I kept saying, ''Breathe, breathe, you silly bitch'' as I pumped away on her chest, but she never did. By the time the ambulance finally got there and took over, I was in tears—tears of anger and frustration.'

Inspector (29 years' service) a 6-month probationer at the time

Dealing with death is part of the job and though it is never pleasant there are times when it can get worse than normal.

> *'I entered the living room and discovered a two-week decomposing body of an elderly gentleman. The body had turned a deep purple in colour, it was extremely bloated, and had started to sink into the living room carpet. The smell was intoxicating and almost to the point I felt dizzy. The facial features were unrecognisable covered by a moving mass of maggots. The situation was so surreal . . .'*
> **PC (6 months' service) working in a medium-sized town**

Of course, if the only thing that police officers got out of the job was the frustrations then, despite the excitement, few would stay in it for long. There are great rewards too.

7.4 **Rewards**

Almost every police officer will tell you that the rewards of 'The Job' far outweigh the frustrations. The panel of serving officers helping with this book were asked, 'What do you enjoy most about the job?' The answers were wide and varied, and much longer than the list of frustrations. The following is a sample of what was said:

> *'Seeing an improvement in the lives of the communities that we police.'*
> **Chief Constable in a county force**

> *'Making a difference. In some small way police officers can affect people's lives for the better and when someone's quality of life is improved by something you have done, it makes it all worthwhile.'*
> **Detective Sergeant in a county force**

'In 29 years there have been very few days when I haven't had at least one good belly laugh at work. How many jobs can you say that about?'
Inspector in a county force

'Being involved in the community and trying to sort out some of the issues. It is a great feeling when you have helped someone, there are still a large majority of people who appreciate and support the work that the police do. After 13 years, I still look forward to going to work, whatever shift I am on.' **PC in a county force**

'The thing I have always enjoyed is the fact that you never know what you will encounter during a tour of duty. No matter how long you have been doing the job you are always learning. I also enjoy the freedom the job gives you, you are making decisions on a daily basis, without being told what to do or always having someone looking over your shoulder.'
Sergeant in a county force

'Watching people commit crime who believe that nobody knows what they are doing and then securing quality convictions. My years in covert policing have proved my most memorable!'
Acting Detective Inspector in a county force

'A real sense of achievement, a simple thank you from a member of the public you have helped is worth its weight in gold.'
PC in a large city force

'Variety, importance, stress, challenging, teamwork, the list is endless. I have looked at my friends in the ''outside world'' and there is no way they can get the same job satisfaction as I get. They might get more money than me, but then that's not everything.'
Sergeant in a county force

'The camaraderie. Whatever position I have had the fortune to have been in, there has always been a sense of team spirit, and, whenever

problems have arisen, whether at work or at home, there has always been someone to talk to.' **PC in a county force**

'...some days it's routine—some days it's anything but!' **PC in a county force**

Great though the rewards are, policing is nothing like it is on television. In the next chapter we will do a brief reality check, but let us conclude this chapter with two specific examples of why the job is 'The Best in The World'.

'I love it when everything comes together. One night I was on my way to an alarm at a club that had been screwed a couple of times, when I saw a man walking in the opposite direction. He looked across but didn't really seem to take any notice of me. There was something that wasn't quite right about him, and I couldn't put my finger on it. I had actually driven past him when I realised what it was—his clothes weren't hanging right and the way he was walking was just odd. I swung the car round and came up behind him, he still didn't take any notice, but I knew I had my grounds for reasonable suspicion. When I searched him all his pockets were full of 10p and 50p pieces and pound coins—he had screwed the club's fruit machines.'

Sergeant (14 years' service) working in a medium-sized town

'...[after the judge had passed sentence] before he went down the steps I looked into his eyes and thought "Yes!".'

Detective Inspector (20 years' service) in
Specialist Investigations

Police work is exciting and boring, satisfying and frustrating. It is ultimately very rewarding. It is, however, nothing like it is portrayed on television and in fiction, or rather there is a lot more to it than is ever shown. In the next chapter we will look at some of those aspects of policing that don't make for a good story.

FURTHER READING

→ David Copperfield, *Wasting Police Time: The Crazy World of the War on Crime*, 2006, Monday Books

8

REALITY CHECK

Research carried out by a university into the motivations of recruits in a county force showed that most of them had got their impressions of what policing was like from television programmes. The reality, as you may well by now have realised, is somewhat far from that projected in programmes like 'The Bill' and 'Traffic Cops'. Experienced trainers have noted some common misapprehensions, facts of life about policing that seem to come as a shock to some recruits and, too often, are the cause of their resignations—to the detriment of everybody involved. So in this chapter we will explore some of those issues.

8.1 Respect for race and diversity

The subject of race and diversity is mentioned several times throughout this book and no apology will be made for emphasising it here. Demonstrating respect for race and diversity is an absolute fundamental in the modern police service and a core duty and is required of every officer and employee.

In Chapter 1 we looked at the attestation and briefly explored the meaning of the phrase, 'according equal respect to all people' that is contained in it. Every force and police authority has a Race Equality Strategy, which commits them to actively promoting equality and fairness both in the workplace and in the communities they serve. In addition most if not all forces will have a statement of values; the one below is from Sussex Police, but it is typical of what you will find in them all:

> *We, the police officers, police staff and volunteers of Sussex Police, are dedicated to the values which underpin police service: integrity, fairness, equity, justice and courage. We will actively build a culture in our Force which is overtly hostile to those who discriminate on the grounds of race, religion, skin colour, sexual orientation, disability, gender, social class or any other inappropriate factor.*

Additionally, as a police officer, you have a duty to treat everyone with fairness and according to their needs as an individual. You should note that treating people the way you would want to be treated is *not* enough.

Before you decide to apply to become a police officer ask yourself if you can sign up to a statement of values similar to the one quoted above. Can you treat everyone with respect and according to their needs as an individual? In deciding your answers, keep in mind what we said in Chapter 1—the rules apply on and off duty. If you can't honestly and sincerely answer yes to both questions you should pursue another line of work, because if you do manage to get into the police your career will be unhappy, and short.

8.2 **Shift work**

Most people realise that policing is a service that is provided for 24 hours every day of the year. Strange as it may seem, not every recruit realises that this means having to work through the night, regardless of one's gender and age. Different forces have different shift patterns, so it is not possible to say here how the work rota is organised for the force you may be interested in joining. What you can be sure of is that there are days when you will be starting early in the morning (0600 or 0700 are common), days when you will be starting in the afternoon (any time between 1400 and 1800) and working through the evening, and days when you will work a night shift (usually starting at 2200 or 2300).

You will notice that no finishing times were given; this was deliberate. Nowadays shifts are usually planned to be ten hours long (eight on night duty). However, what is planned and what actually happens are all too frequently different things. If you have arrested someone or are otherwise involved in a job, you will generally be required to stay on duty until you have either finished all that needs to be done for the time being or you have got to the point that the job can be handed on to someone else *and* there is someone else to hand it on to (by no means a forgone conclusion, particularly in county forces). You will not have a choice in this and it means that you will frequently be late getting home, sometimes by many hours. Of course, when you are late in finishing it doesn't mean that your shift the following day will start any later; generally, unless you worked for more than about 18 hours, you will be expected to turn up for work at the normal time.

You may be thinking that, though it might be tiring during the week, you will at least have your days off to recover and be with your family. Well that is not actually guaranteed. The fact is that a police officer is obliged to work when required and if your force needs you to work on your days off then, unless you resign, you have no choice but to do so. I should say that all hours worked in excess of those normally rostered do attract overtime compensation; the rules on this are too complex to go into here. The long, anti-social and unpredictable hours are frequently a cause of domestic disharmony (there will be many missed birthdays, anniversary dinners and children's plays) and divorce amongst police officers is, regrettably, common.

Another cause of domestic strife is the officer's emotional state on getting home. Policing is, as you have seen, an occupation that generates a great deal of stress, frustration and other negative emotions, but while you are working, the need to be professional means that you have to keep your emotions under strict control. Therefore, there is the temptation to want to unload on your partner when you finally get home, at whatever hour of the day. If not done too often there is not generally a problem, but continually 'taking the job home' is a sure-fire way to make your partner extremely unhappy and to damage your relationship (wise police officers know this and will have developed a way of 'dumping work' before going home).

If you are serious about joining the police and are in a long-term relationship you would be well advised to discuss what it is likely to mean for both of you and make sure that you are both happy to deal with it.

8.3 Dealing with confrontation

Dealing with confrontation is an everyday occurrence for every street-duty police officer. Getting people to do what you want them to do is a very large part of the job. There are an awful lot of people who won't want to oblige you and will tell you so, to the point of violence. There are also people who will hate you simply because of the uniform you are wearing.

In Chapter 10 you will find out that you will be expertly trained in how to deal with confrontation and prove your competence in those skills before you are allowed out on the streets. However, make no mistake about it, there will be times when you will have to tell people directly what you want them to do and, if necessary, make them do it. You will be shouted at, sworn at and spat on, and, regardless of the training you have received, you will be thumped. If you go into any police station in England and Wales you will not find anyone who has been an active street-duty police officer who has not been physically attacked on duty. Your training will reduce the frequency and, hopefully, lessen the potential seriousness, but you will be assaulted at some stage.

As with other things we have mentioned if you are not sure that you are prepared to deal with confrontation and violence then it will be best if you did not pursue a career in the police.

8.4 **Workload**

This was hinted at this in previous chapters, but it's worth being explicit about; the days of the old-fashioned foot patrol where the PC walked the beat, meeting and chatting to residents and looking out for what was happening and dealing with it as necessary, have pretty much gone. Unless it is part of a targeted operation very few officers now even have the chance of foot patrol. There is too much to do and the performance culture demands results that can be counted. An example will illustrate the pressure PCs are now under.

EXAMPLE

This is the second 'burglary dwelling' I have been to this morning and I have an assault to go to next. I have got 16 other crimes in my tray that I am supposed to be investigating, no idea how I am supposed to do that.

PC (2 years' service) working in a small town

That young PC, by the way, was the only one on duty that morning in an area covering a couple of dozen square miles including a town with a population of nearly 30,000 people. If you are wondering about back-up in case he got into difficulties, so was he.

Even aside from the stress engendered when dealing with some individual incidents, the sheer volume of work, and the need to deliver results, places a lot of pressure on the street-duty police officers.

8.5 **Why people stay**

Unlike the armed forces, there are no terms of engagement for the police; it is not necessary to sign up for a set number of years. It is possible to resign at any time simply by giving 28 days' notice. Despite everything, most people who join stay in for a full career. These are some of the reasons given for staying in:

'I got hooked from the word go. I made close friends and I felt I was making a difference.' **Chief Constable of a county force**

'Every day was different, every challenge a new challenge, every stumbling block a bridge to cross. And I was guaranteed a good wage and I was unlikely to be made redundant!' **PC in a large city force**

'There have been a number of times during my career where I have questioned, am I doing the right thing? Or there must be better jobs around? However, in all the jobs I have had before becoming a police officer, I have never had a job that on one hand can be so rewarding and the next so thankless. I think it's that, that keeps me coming back for more.' **PC in a county force**

'I stayed because I couldn't think of another type of work in which I could make such a direct difference to people in so many different ways.' **PC in a county force**

'The job has had its highs and lows over 20 years. On occasion it has been "quite brutal", but what has kept me going on all occasions has been the companionship of my colleagues.' **Sergeant in a county force**

'There is just so much different work to be done. There are lots of different departments and different types of work. The police do become your

family and so it is difficult to just give it up. There is always something new to do and I like that and so am happy to stay. Even after 26 years I still love coming to work and actually am worried about when I have to give up!!' **Detective Inspector in a county force**

'Because of the variety of work within the job. The ability to work on shifts and beats, in rural areas and city centres, to teach and train, to be attached to crime units and a multitude of other departments.'
PC in a county force

'Being a professional police officer is extremely satisfying. You feel that you are making a difference to the world.'
Detective Chief Inspector in a county force

This chapter has not been written to put anybody off joining the police. Like the rest of the book, it is intended to inform potential police officers what 'The Job' is actually about and what doing it entails. It is much better for everybody if new recruits come in with their eyes wide open and knowing what to expect. The subject of joining the police is the focus of the next part of the book. There we will look at the recruiting process and the training new officers are given.

FURTHER READING

→ <http://www.archive.official-documents.co.uk/document/cm42/4262/4262.htm>
Here you will find the full text of the Macpherson Report, the finding of the enquiry into the police actions connected with the murder of Stephen Lawrence. This report has had a massive impact on how the police carry out their duties, yet it is one of the misquoted and misunderstood documents of recent history. If you are serious about a career in the police you should take time to read this report in full.

PART III

RECRUITING AND TRAINING

9

THE SELECTION PROCESS

As you will probably have realised by now, if you did not know it already, being a police officer is not an easy job and it is not a job that a lot of people *can* do. There are about 8,000 recruits taken on across England and Wales each year; there are more than 50,000 applicants. You should not let that statistic put you off trying; a great many applications are turned down, not because the person didn't have what it takes, but because they did not understand the recruiting system and so failed to demonstrate their potential for the job. In this chapter we will look at the selection process and how it works.

9.1 **Would I fit in?**

Before we look at the process itself it will probably be useful to deal with a question asked by a great many people thinking of joining, 'Would I fit in?' As you will have seen from the previous chapters, policing deals with a wide variety of issues in the community—and it needs an equally wide variety of individuals to do it. If you think back to Peel's Principles of Policing that we looked at in Chapter 2, it was clearly set down that if the Service is to be effective then 'the police are the public and the public are the police' must be true; in other words the make-up of the force must reflect the make-up of the communities it serves. Whilst this has yet to be fully achieved, it is true to say that officers from all different cultural, social, religious and ethnic backgrounds train and work alongside each other.

In a report called 'Training Matters' (which we will meet formally in Chapter 10) Her Majesty's Inspector of Constabulary said:

> Few other professions place so much importance on the way their members interact with customers and each other.

You should note the last phrase, 'and each other'. Teamwork is fundamental to modern policing and a fellow officer's background is irrelevant, all that matters is whether they can do the job.

Every police force has a well publicised equal opportunities policy that sets out the way in which individuals can expect to be treated. Of course, the strict legal requirements which make it unlawful to discriminate against anyone because of their sex, race, married status, age, religious belief, sexual orientation or any other inappropriate factor apply just as much to the police as any other job. But forces' equal opportunities policies go further than that, they go further than guaranteeing your right to be treated equally; as we saw in Chapter 8, you will find that the policy actively promotes a non-discriminatory culture.

So the answer to the question 'Would I fit in?' is quite simple. Do you meet the minimum standards in relation to physical fitness, character and so on (these can be found on the Home Office website <http://www.policecouldyou.co.uk>) and can you pass the selection process? If the answer to both of these is yes, then you could fit right in.

9.2 **The paper sift**

The first stage of the selection process is assessing the application forms; most applications that fail do so at this point. You can download an application form from the 'police could you' website given above. You might want to do this to see what would be expected of you.

There are three main reasons why some applicants who could make good police officers fail at this stage. The first reason is that they didn't fill in the application form in accordance with the instructions. It may sound obvious but, given the number of applicants who clearly don't, it has to be mentioned here; do read the guidance notes for completion before you start to fill the form in. Pay particular attention to the section on competency assessment.

The second reason is poor spelling, punctuation, grammar and general presentation. As it says in the notes, these are assessed throughout the form. If you make more than a couple of spelling mistakes your application will be rejected.

The third reason is that the applicant fails to demonstrate the skills and competencies that the process is looking for in the competency assessment section. This doesn't mean that they don't have them; simply that they didn't demonstrate them on the form. Unfortunately, confidentiality precludes details of how these questions are scored being included here but there are some things that can be said.

The questions that most people fall down on are the first four. Look at the headings of these:

Q1 It is vitally important that police officers show respect for others, irrespective of their background.

Q2 Police officers often work in teams and it is important that you are able to work well with others, and are willing to share in the less attractive jobs.

Q3 Police officers often need to remain calm and act logically and decisively in very difficult circumstances.

Q4 Police officers have to be able to communicate with a wide range of people, both verbally and in writing.

In each case you have to provide an example from your life relating to the topic. If you look you can see where the assessors are going, namely:

- Q1 — respect for race and diversity
- Q2 — team working
- Q3 — resilience
- Q4 — effective communication

Furthermore when you look at the some of the questions, for each that you are asked to answer, you can see that they are also looking for evidence in relation to:

- personal responsibility
- problem solving
- community and customer focus

These seven things are the core behaviours that police officers are expected to have and to develop. It is worth looking at them in a little detail.

Respect for race and diversity

Understands other people's views and takes them into account. Is tactful and diplomatic when dealing with people. Treats people with dignity and respect at all times, no matter what their background, status, circumstances or appearance.

Team working

Works effectively as a team member and helps build relationships with the team. Actively helps and supports others to achieve team goals.

Resilience

Shows reliability and resilience in difficult circumstances. Remains calm and confident, and responds logically and decisively in difficult situations.

Effective communication

Communicates all needs, instructions and decisions clearly. Adapts the style of communication to meet the needs of the audience. Asks probing questions to check understanding.

Personal responsibility

Takes personal responsibility for own actions and for sorting out issues or problems that arise. Is focused on achieving results to required standards and developing skills and knowledge.

Problem solving

Gathers enough relevant information to understand specific issues and events. Uses information to identify problems and draw logical conclusions. Makes good decisions.

Community and customer focus

Provides a high level of service to customers. Maintains contact with customers, works out what they need and responds to them. Is aware of issues of diversity, and understands and is sensitive to cultural and racial differences.

Applicants who provide evidence to demonstrate the above behaviours don't fail the competency assessment. Of course, space is limited and you will not be able to show every trait from one example, but the more you can show the better. Armed with this information you may want to look at the sample answer given in the guidance notes and see how the author has worked in the core behaviours.

Meeting the requirements of the paper sift is not particularly difficult if you think about it and work out your answers carefully.

9.3 **The assessment centre**

When you are through the paper sift you will be invited to the next stage of the selection process, a one day assessment centre. With your invitation will come an information pack which details how the day will run and, crucially, the competencies that will be tested—together with the positive and negative behaviour indicators for each (i.e. those things that the assessors are wanting to hear and those things that, if you produce too many of them, will result in you failing). Most, if not all, forces also provide a pre-event briefing for candidates. Experienced assessors have said that it is very unusual to fail the assessment centre if you prepare for it properly.

During the day you will take part in four assessed activities:

- a numerical reasoning test;
- a verbal reasoning/literacy test;
- an interview;
- a series of four interactive role plays.

There is not much that can be said about the numerical reasoning test other than if you have Adult Level 2 or GCSE mathematics you should not have a problem with it. The others could usefully do with some detailed description here.

Literacy test

In this test you will be given a briefing sheet which details a problem. Your task is to draft a letter in response. As with the application form, clear, concise and grammatically correct English is a must. In particular if you make more than five spelling mistakes you will fail. Other than that a logical structure and a reasoned proposed course of action that addresses the problem should see you clear.

Interview

This interview will be like no other one you have ever had or, probably, ever will have. It lasts for 20 minutes and the single assessor will ask you four questions. He or she will read the questions from a script and each one will be prefixed by the competency that is being assessed. You will have five minutes to answer the question. During your answer the assessor will be listening for the behaviour indicators for the relevant competency and marking them on a score card, so they will not make any eye contact with you or give any sort of feedback (no nodding of the head or 'ah ha' noises that are part of everyday communication). If you come to the end of your answer before the five minutes is up the assessor may ask you if you have finished and if you have they will move on to the next question. On the other hand if you are still talking at the five minute mark the assessor will cut you off and move on to the next question.

The reason for this unusual structure is to ensure that every candidate is treated exactly the same and so the process is as fair as it possibly can be. There is, however, no doubt that it can seem to be a cold and artificial way of conducting an interview. It is very difficult to talk to the top of someone's head, especially when you are getting no feedback from the person at all. It is not unknown for unprepared candidates to dry up after a sentence or two for each answer and then they and the assessor have to sit in silence until the 20 minutes is up.

The information pack will tell you what competencies will be tested and what the positive behaviour indictors are. So, well before the day, for each competency, think of two examples from any part of your life (work, home, school, university, armed services—it doesn't matter) and rehearse them. Even go so far as to write down what you are going to say and learn it by heart. Make sure that you check your lines against the behaviour indicators. Then in the interview listen for the competency to be tested in the question and explain *both* your prepared examples for it—always give two examples, that way you can cover more of the behaviours.

The only other thing to remember is, especially if the question is about teamwork, don't say 'we', as in, 'We did such and such', 'We solved the problem by...' Always say 'I'; it is you that is being assessed not the team.

The interview might be cold and artificial but, if you have prepared for it, it is the easiest of the activities.

Interactive role play

You will do four interactive role plays, or, if you prefer, role exercises. At every assessment centre held so far they have been based around a fictional shopping centre and the candidate plays the role of the customer services manager—there is no reason to suspect that this will change in the future. You start at the preparation station for your first exercise. There you will find a briefing sheet and you will have five minutes to read it; you are allowed to make notes. At the end of five minutes a buzzer will sound and you will move to the door of the actual event. After 90 seconds the buzzer will sound again and in you go. Inside will be a role actor—the person that is mentioned in the briefing—and standing in the corner behind you, and out of your line of view, will be the assessor. The role actor will give you the first line and you have five minutes to deal with the situation, whatever it may be. At the end of that time the buzzer will go again and the actor will immediately stop talking, the assessment will be over and you will move on to the preparation station for the next exercise.

The role actor has a briefing; it will tell him or her the demeanour that he or she is to take (nervous, arrogant, angry etc.) and the 14 lines he or she is allowed to say. No matter what you say, or how the situation develops, they will never say anything other than one of those 14 lines.

Some people find role plays difficult and, unlike the interview, there is not a lot you can do in preparation. If this applies to you, then you might want to think about where and how you could practise getting into a role and behaving the way you would if you were a customer services manager of a shopping centre. It will be fatal to your chances of success if you walked into the room and had an attack of the giggles or otherwise didn't start demonstrating your competencies straight away—you need to fill the five minutes with quality.

As ever, competencies are being tested in this activity and you will need to show the behaviour traits. Good people fail here not because they can't do it but because they don't show what is being looked for. To give an example, if the competency being assessed is problem solving you will need to show that you gather information to understand the problem, consider possible options that logically follow from the information you have gathered and then choose one that makes some sort of sense to the assessor. If you merely listen to the problem and then announce a solution you will score very badly, no matter how good your solution is.

Other points to remember are:

- listen to the actor, really listen to what they say;

- do not use jargon, particularly police jargon;

- do not try to deal with the situation as if you were a police officer;

- ignore the assessor;

- when you have finished a role play, wipe it from your mind;

- never point your finger at the actor or use other confrontational or inappropriate body language—you will fail if you do.

To finish this section on the assessment centre, there are some general points that may be of use. First of all your behaviour is monitored all of the time and not just in the assessed activities. You will instantly fail if:

- you use inappropriate language (racist or sexist comments etc.);
- your conduct in any activity is hopelessly wide of the mark;
- you talk so softly or indistinctly you cannot be heard or understood;
- your communication makes no sense.

There is no dress code for the assessment centre; how you look forms no part of the assessment. However, one of the things that most definitely will be tested is your ability to communicate effectively. When we are talking, the listener only gets 7 per cent of the message from what we actually say; another 35 per cent comes from how we say it and the rest—the majority—comes from our body language. How you are dressed is part of that body language. The only thing that will be scored is what you say (the 7 per cent). However, the assessors are only human and your appearance will have an impact and that *may* affect your score and that *may* mean the difference between pass and fail.

For each activity the assessor will have something that looks like a large version of the form you fill in when buying a national lottery ticket. On it will be a line for each behaviour trait for the competency being tested; for each trait you will be marked on whether you demonstrate it and if so how well. At the end of the assessment centre your score cards will be sent to a national centre where they will be computer marked together with all the candidates from across the country and a standardised score will be produced. At the time of writing (summer 2006) the pass mark is 60 per cent, though this may from time to time be changed—it was previously 50 per cent. You will be sent your result two weeks after the assessment centre.

9.4 **The fitness test**

If you pass the assessment centre the last hurdle (other than the medical and reference checks, which needn't detain us here) is the fitness test. A lot of applicants worry about this, but unless they are grossly unfit they shouldn't. It is nowhere near as hard as people think—indeed, to prove a point, a sergeant in his 40s recently successfully completed it whilst smoking a cigarette. The fitness test consists of three activities:

- the shuttle run
- the push test
- the pull test.

In the shuttle run, candidates must run up and down a 15 metre track for at least a set time (currently three and half minutes for men and two minutes forty-five seconds for women). Each 15 metre run must be completed before a buzzer sounds; as the test goes on, the interval between buzzes gets progressively shorter, so the candidate must run faster.

The push and pull tests are done sitting at a machine. The candidate has three goes at pulling a spring-loaded bar towards him or her and three goes at pushing it away. A meter built into the machine records the strength of the push and pull and for each at least one of the three attempts must reach a certain level. However, the pass mark is sufficiently low that a normal, averagely fit adult can achieve it without too much difficulty.

The statistics indicate that getting into the Service is not easy—only about 15 per cent of applicants are successful. However, as you have seen, providing you actually have the personal attributes that are being sought, some sound preparation at each stage will reduce the odds dramatically. Of course, getting in is only the start; you also have to complete the training successfully and we will look at what that means in the next chapter.

FURTHER READING

→ <http://www.policecouldyou.co.uk>

→ H. Tolley, C. Tolley, B. Hodge, *How to Pass the New Police Selection System*, 2004, Kogan Page

→ S. Sutcliffe & W. Francis, *Passing the Police Recruit Assessment Process*, 2007, Law Matters Publishing

→ C.J. Tyreman, *Police Initial Recruitment Test (Mock Test With Preparation)*, 2003, ELC Publications

10

INITIAL TRAINING

Once you have got through the selection process you will be sent a letter offering you an appointment to your force. It is usually somewhere around three months before you actually begin your new career, but that day will eventually come when you turn up at the force headquarters or training centre to start learning how to do 'The Job'. In this chapter we will look at the sort of training you will receive and how you will be assessed.

First of all a note of caution: as you have seen there are more than 40 police forces in England and Wales and despite the standardisation that has been going on over recent years they are all proudly unique and have their own traditions and, in particular, they do not all use the same terminology. In this book we try to use only standard terms, but don't be surprised if, when you talk to individual forces, they use different names for the roles, tasks and processes that you will read about below.

10.1 **Probation**

The first thing to note about initial police training is that it extends for a two-year period and during that time you will be on probation. You may recall that in Chapter 4 we looked at what that meant. The term 'probationer' is now going out of fashion—to be replaced by 'student officer', but the change of name does not alter the fact that you will be on probation.

Having recalled our discussion in Chapter 4, you will probably remember that it will be your task to prove that you can do 'The Job'. We will look at what that means in practice later on, when we consider how you will be assessed during your training, but right now there is a very important fact you need to know about—it is called 'Regulation 13'.

We saw in Chapter 1 that as a constable you will not have a contract of employment and at least some employment law will not apply to you. Instead your life on duty and off will be governed by the Code of Conduct and Police Regulations. Whilst you are on probation Regulation 13 is important. What it says is:

> ... during his period of probation in the force the services of a constable may be dispensed with at any time if the chief officer considers that he is not fitted, physically or mentally, to perform the duties of his office, or that he is not likely to become an efficient or well conducted constable.

What this means is that if your conduct (on duty or off) or your performance is unacceptable you can be fired. Probationers have been sacked for dishonest behaviour that, in other occupations, probably would not even merit a written warning. Drunken behaviour off-duty, particularly when it is likely to bring discredit on the force, has also seen a fair number of probationers face dismissal under this regulation. A bad sickness record could, quite likely, lead the force to decide that the officer is physically unsuited to 'The Job' and get rid of him or her. However, failing to meet the standards required in training is the biggest cause of Regulation 13 being invoked.

You should not be unduly alarmed about this regulation; no force wants to lose people in whom, even during their early training, they have invested considerable sums. Except in cases of unacceptable conduct, Regulation 13 is never used without warning. Officers who are struggling will always be given lots of help and support, but at the end of the day there is no room for someone who cannot meet the grade. There is no appeal to an employment tribunal for a dismissal under Regulation 13, though the officer can apply to the courts for a judicial review of the decision.

10.2 Initial Police Learning and Development Programme

The Initial Police Learning and Development Programme (IPLDP) is the national standard for the training of new officers during their first two years of training and was introduced across England and Wales in April 2006, though a few forces had been piloting it up to 15 months beforehand.

Previously, initial training had followed the same path since at least the end of the Second World War. After a short induction period at their Force Training School, recruits were sent off to a District Training Centre for a residential course lasting 12 weeks (the course had been as short as 10 weeks and as long as 15). There, in company with recruits from other forces in the region, they were schooled in the basics of law and procedure, with role play exercises carried out on site to enable them to practise their new skills and knowledge.

On returning to their force the recruits went through a local procedure course intended to get them up to speed with their own force's way of doing things. Then they went to their stations and worked with an experienced constable to tutor them for up to 10 weeks, before finally being released to work on their own. Short training courses were attended during the remainder of the two years to deliver more new law knowledge and refresh what they had learned at the District Training Centre.

On the whole this training regime worked reasonably well and was enjoyed by just about everyone involved. However, it did have some serious weaknesses and as the years wore on these were becoming more and more apparent. What had been ideal in the 1940s, and more than acceptable in the 1970s, was, by the mid-1990s, struggling. Society had changed dramatically since 1946 and not only had society's expectations of the police changed with it, so too had the needs of the recruits.

In 2000/01 Her Majesty's Inspectorate of Constabulary carried out a thematic inspection of police training. Their report not only picked up on the weaknesses of the existing training of recruits, it condemned it as 'unfit for purpose'. (The report was called 'Training Matters' and it is available on the HMIC website. If you really want to understand police training, it is a worthwhile read.)

Training Matters was, fortuitously, published in early 2002 at a time when the Home Office was starting the Police Reform Programme, and a new initial training regime could form a key plank in the modernisation of the workforce. Working groups, which included all interested parties, were set up to consider the way forward and by 2003 two vital decisions had been made:

- the new arrangements would comply with a Learning Requirement that had just been finalised;

- forces would be free to implement their own training arrangements provided they met the Learning Requirement and certain key principles.

Although there was a lot of work to be done, IPLDP was born.

10.3 Current training regime

As the current training regime has some minimum standards but otherwise allows forces to implement a training programme that best suits their own needs and the needs of the communities they serve, you will by now have guessed that, with 46 forces, there are 46 different training programmes. Therefore, it is impossible to be exact about the training that you will undergo. What we can do is look at the mandatory features that will be common to all and look at the different styles of training that are on offer.

National Occupational Standards

To ensure that every officer, no matter what force they join, achieves a minimum standard of capability to do the job, all student officers must demonstrate competence in 22 National Occupational Standards (NOSs).

National Occupational Standards have been developed by the Skills for Justice agency in conjunction with representatives from chief officers, police authorities and community partners. They provide a method of assessing competent performance in terms of the tasks to be achieved in the workplace. If you have ever worked for an NVQ quali- fication you will be familiar with this sort of competence measuring.

Each of the 22 standards has one or more elements which in turn have specific tasks—competence in which must be demonstrated (known as performance criteria). This may sound complex but, once you get the hang of it, it is actually quite straightforward. We will look at how the assessment of competence is done later on in this chapter. There is not the space in this book to set down the rele- vant NOSs but you can find them on the Skills for Justice website (<http://www.skillsforjustice.net/nos/with-ple.htm>).

Stages: basic training and independent patrol

The time a student officer spends on probation is divided into two parts, the basic training period and independent patrol.

Basic training is the period when the new officer learns the funda- mental skills and knowledge that will enable them to perform street duty on their own; in the next section we will look at what this involves. The length of time that this period of learning takes varies from force to force, the shortest would appear to be 26 weeks and the longest is

52 weeks. Before an officer can be signed off to work on their own, they have to show that they are competent in 11 key areas of day-to-day policing. This list of competencies is known as the Police Action Checklist (PAC).

Once they have been granted independent patrol, student officers join an operational section in the police station to which they have been posted and work as a regular member of the team. In this time they will continue to show their competence against the 22 NOSs and must by the end of the two years have got all of them signed off. They will, generally, also undergo periods of additional formal training. The amount of time that is devoted to this seems to depend on the length of the basic training and it varies from more than six weeks to none at all.

One interesting thing to note about police training is that student officers on independent patrol, although they have not finished their training, much less shown that they are competent in all the areas necessary for a fully fledged police officer, are treated just like any other street-duty PC. They are sent to calls as they come in and are expected, at least by the public, to cope with whatever the job throws at them. One officer on her very first day out on her own was the first at the scene of a stranger-rape and had to deal with the situation, the scene and a very distressed victim for a considerable period before more experienced help could get there.

Key elements

However a force organises its basic training and however long it takes it will contain some key elements and we will look at these now.

Induction

The training will start with an induction period. This will probably be quite short and is designed to introduce you to the force and the training programme. You will be issued with your uniform (and taught how to wear it) and 'sworn in' as a constable (remember the attestation in Chapter 1).

Classroom learning

Student officers have to learn a great deal of law, policy and procedure. Although some of this can and will be absorbed in the workplace, there is no substitute for a safe learning environment. In most cases the training will be delivered by experienced police officers who hold recognised training qualifications. In some forces, especially those who are working in partnership with a university, some of the training is carried out by lecturers who have the specialist knowledge required. Regardless of who is delivering it, you will find that in modern police training there are very few old-fashioned chalk-and-talk lessons. Sessions are designed to be interactive and to ensure that all students learn as much as they can.

In most forces the classroom learning takes place on police premises, usually the force training school, but others have their student officers on a university campus integrated with the wider student community. In all but one or two forces, basic training is not residential and the classroom element takes place during the normal working day—that is to say nine to five from Monday to Friday.

Staff safety training

Staff safety training is about the skills, both verbal and physical, necessary to deal with violent conflict with the least chance of getting hurt and using the minimum force necessary. In some forces this is known as Unarmed Defence Technique (UDT) training. It includes how to use a baton properly and the correct use of incapacitant spray. All officers are required to qualify in these skills before they can set foot on the street as an operational officer. You won't, by now, be surprised to learn that the length (and content) of the training varies from force to force, but the average length of time seems to be about eight days.

Workplace learning

Workplace learning, sometimes called supervised patrol, is when the new officer takes to the streets in the company of a tutor constable to put into practice the knowledge and skills learned in the classroom and to learn more, both directly and indirectly. In some forces this takes place in one continuous block at the end of a lengthy period of classroom-based training (like the old, pre-IPLDP style of training); in others, periods in the classroom and periods in the workplace are interleaved and the activities in the latter are carefully directed to help achieve set learning outcomes. During this phase of your training you can expect to be working something close to normal shift patterns, including weekend working.

Community placements

One of the problems identified with the old style of initial police training was that it all took place in a closed police environment and new officers didn't learn about the communities they were to police. Now all officers are required to spend a minimum of 80 hours in community placements. Depending on the needs of the force, this time can be spent in short visits to learn something of community customs and needs (e.g. a day spent with the imam at a local mosque) and/or longer periods actually working in and with a community group (e.g. a needle exchange scheme).

Community placements are being seen as successful in helping to break down barriers between the police and some parts of society and also improving the officers' abilities to police sensitively, taking into account the needs of individuals.

Assessment

As a student officer you have to demonstrate your competence to do 'The Job'. If you don't, as we have seen, you will lose your job. This simple fact is at the heart of the assessment process — the student must prove themselves. To ensure that this process is fair and open each student officer will keep a portfolio of evidence as they progress through their training. In most forces this is known as the SOLAP or Student Officer Learning Assessment Portfolio, and if you have ever worked for an NVQ you will be quite at home with the process.

To prove competence in a PAC or NOS the student has to produce evidence. This can be in the form of a witness testament from a qualified officer who saw the student demonstrate the required behaviour or it can be documents which in themselves show what is required (in some cases the SOLAP will only contain a reference number as the original document will be of operational importance — e.g. a crime file). On a regular basis each student's SOLAP will be examined by a qualified assessor and if they agree that evidence is sufficient the relevant performance criteria will be signed off in the SOLAP. The work of the assessor will be subsequently checked by one or more qualified verifiers to ensure standards are maintained and equal across the force area. Just so you know, the work of the verifier will be dip-checked by an external verifier to ensure that standards across forces are equal.

In addition to the evidence for the NOSs the SOLAP will contain a record of the student's assessment against theoretical knowledge; that is to say, how well they know the law, policies and procedure that they have been required to learn. Whilst the assessment of NOSs is standardised across England and Wales, how the students' theoretical knowledge is measured varies from force to force. Some use formal examinations (generally of the multiple-choice style), some use essays and written projects, some use a mixture of both.

The SOLAP will also contain notes of tutorial meetings and such action plans as are agreed to help the student officer develop. Finally, it will contain a learning diary or reflective journal. We will look at this in some detail in the next chapter, so we can leave it for now.

Qualifications

Twice in this chapter it has been mentioned that the process involved in initial training is very similar to that of an NVQ, and we have also mentioned the agency Skills for Justice who are involved in NVQs elsewhere in the public sector. You may now be wondering if completing your initial training will lead to the award of a nationally recognised qualification. The answer to that is yes.

Some forces have geared their initial training so that their student officers will, when they finish their probation, have qualified for both a Level 3 and a Level 4 NVQ in Policing. Others stay at level 3. Some other forces have entered into partnership arrangements with a local university, and the completion of basic training (i.e. achieving independent patrol) will lead to the award of a Certificate in Higher Education—the equivalent of the first year of an honours degree course. Of these forces, some offer student officers the opportunity to study for and achieve a Foundation Degree before they finish probation, and at least one force insists that they do. It is likely that the Government will ensure that there is a single minimum qualification for student officers. This will probably be the Level 3 NVQ. However, forces that offer the university route have programmes that will qualify their people for this award without any significant change.

The key point to remember about initial police training is that it is really about getting you up to the standards that are needed. There is no sudden death. If, when you submit your SOLAP, the assessor doesn't agree that you have sufficient evidence for a particular performance criterion, it is not an instant fail. They will tell you why and what you need to do. This is not a pass or fail process, it is a developmental process. Nobody will expect you to do the job perfectly first time out, your senior officers will expect you to make mistakes and get it wrong.

The only time this becomes a problem (and so leads to Regulation 13) is when you don't learn from your mistakes—and we will look at how to avoid that in the next chapter.

FURTHER READING

→ <http://www.policecouldyou.co.uk>

→ <http://www.skillsforjustice.com>

11

EXPERIENCE AND REFLECT

If you have ever watched a baby teaching itself to walk you will know that the process involves an awful lot of falling down. After each fall the child picks itself up and tries again and eventually masters walking. There are two interesting things about this. Firstly, there is no 'failure'; lack of success does not stop the soon-to-be-toddler from finally achieving their goal. Secondly, there seems to be something going on that could be verbalised as, 'That didn't work, so perhaps if I tried doing this' and 'That was much better but maybe if I repeated that and did this as well'. Young children do it naturally and it works very well, it's fast, effective and, if not pain-free (there are usually some tears along the way), it is a lot easier than other methods of learning to do complex things. This is directly applicable to police training.

How we teach ourselves as young children, and in our first two years we probably learn more than we do in the rest of our lives, has been given the academic label of 'experiential learning' by psychologists who write learned theses on how and why it works. The models and explanations produced are actually very interesting, but, as you are reading this book because you are interested in being a police officer and not an educational psychologist, we will use a model that has been translated from the academic to the practical—'what, so what and now what'.

11.1 **The experiential learning cycle**

The experiential learning cycle is actually very simple—it is based on two fundamental principles:

• there is no failure, only feedback;
• for any experience, learn from it and move on.

It will help to explain the process if we have a diagram to refer to—see Figure 11.1.

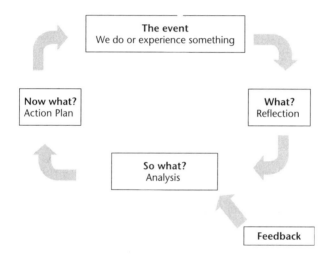

Figure 11.1 The experiential learning cycle

The first thing to note is that there is no beginning and no end—it is a *cycle*. The second key point is that, aside from the event itself, there are three stages. To learn from the experience each stage has to be completed and completed in order. So let's look at them in turn.

What?

The first thing to do is to work out *exactly* what happened. At this stage we are not worried about why things turned out the way they did, we just need to fully understand what really happened. So here you need to 'replay the video', run through in your mind exactly what happened and in what sequence. There is a natural tendency to want to skip the nasty bits, or to alter the experience and try to fool yourself that it went differently, but, if you want to learn, this has to be overcome—you have to be honest with yourself. One way of doing this is to start at the beginning of the event and ask yourself 'What happened next?', and repeat this until you get to the end of the event.

So what?

Now that you understand exactly what happened it is time to decide why things happened as they did; and 'Why?' is the question you need to be asking yourself. 'Why did the person react that way when I said such and such?' 'Why did I do that?' 'Why didn't that work?' 'Why, in the interview, did the burglar decide to admit all those other offences?' This last question illustrates an important point; you use experiential learning after events that went really well, not just with those that seemed to go badly. That way you can learn what you are good at and what to do next time, but that is to jump ahead. The more specific and detailed you make your questions the greater the learning will be.

When you are working with your tutor constable he or she will often go through this process with you after you have dealt with an incident or do a particular task—a process known in the trade as 'Taking them round the ELC' (ELC is short for experiential learning cycle). Your tutor will get you to reflect so you understand the 'what' and then get you to analyse to achieve the 'so what'. At this stage, and only at this stage, will a competent tutor provide feedback and only then if you are not coming to the understanding of the 'why' for yourself. Feedback is someone else's view of the 'why' (and it is always based on their view of the 'what') and, if they are experienced and wise, it is useful to have, but the learning is much deeper and more profound if you come to the conclusions for yourself.

Now what?

At this point, now that you understand why things happened as they did, you can decide what you are going to do in the future when faced with similar circumstances. Here it is just as important to recognise what you did that worked, as well as what you did that did not achieve the result you wanted. You will want to repeat the first and change the second, but even if it went well you will want to look at ways where you could do even better (once a baby learns to walk, they are still a toddler, unsure on their feet, and they still need to master running). The greatest learning comes from taking yourself 'round the ELC' after every experience, making sure you are objective, and honest with yourself.

11.2 **The endless staircase to excellence**

You may be thinking that the ELC is both complex and time consuming and therefore using it after each experience is impossible. Well, yes and no. There is certainly a lot to the ELC, but using it is a skill, and learning a skill takes time and practice but it does become easier and easier until you reach a point where you don't really have to think about it. Let's explore that idea in more depth.

If you have a driving licence you may well remember your early lessons. You will, perhaps, remember the confusion you felt at coming up to a junction? Check the mirror, turn on the indicator, slow down, change gear, steer the car into the right position on the road, check the mirror again—probably, like most people, you felt like you did not have enough hands and could have done with an extra foot. You knew what you needed to do (which you didn't before you started your lessons) but you couldn't do it. However, you wanted the benefits that having a driving licence would bring to your life (freedom, increased mobility, perhaps more career choices) so you persevered and actually, quite quickly, it became easier. Then came the time after you passed your test; you could drive competently, but you had to concentrate to do so. You may remember that time—perhaps most characteristically summed up in the phrase, 'Don't talk to me while I am driving'. You knew what you had to do and could do it, but only with conscious effort. With more practice you have probably reached the point where the mere act of driving is almost automatic, you certainly don't have to think about it. You can drive whilst listening to the radio, having a conversation with the front seat passenger, and maybe yelling at the kids in the back. While it may be controversial in some police circles to admit it, driving has become an unconscious skill. So learning to drive can be thought of as having four steps:

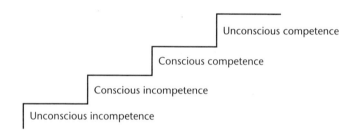

Unconscious competence

Conscious competence

Conscious incompetence

Unconscious incompetence

Figure 11.2 The competence staircase

At the outset you are unconsciously incompetent—you don't even know what it is you need to do, much less be able to do it. Then comes the stage of conscious incompetence—now you know what you must do but can't do it. With practice you master the required skill but you have to think about it—conscious competence. Finally, you reach the stage of unconscious competence—you can do it without having to think about it.

Now, if you join the Service there will come a time, probably after a couple of years, when you will be sent to the force driving school to qualify to drive police cars as a response vehicle driver. There you will meet some of the bravest men and women in the country who, day after day, teach police officers how to drive fast but safely on public roads; this takes real courage. They will show you that, when it comes to driving cars, there are methods and systems that you never even dreamed about. In other words, they will show you that as far as skill behind a wheel goes you are, despite your unconscious competence, in fact unconsciously *incompetent*—there is a whole new level that you didn't know about. During your driving course you will become consciously competent in those new skills. Later on in your career, if you aspire to road policing or take a job that needs surveillance skills, you will go back to the driving school and find out that there is yet another level in driving skill that you knew nothing about.

We have used driving as an example (and traffic officers would probably blanch at the idea that we drive 'automatically') but the example holds true for learning any new skill; no matter how good you are, you can always get better. The fastest and easiest way of improving a skill is to take yourself round the ELC each time you use it; and of course using the ELC is a skill in itself. So if you keep using it, going through the 'what', 'so what' and 'now what' will become second nature and very, very quick to do.

11.3 **Learning diaries**

As a student officer you will be required to keep a 'learning diary', sometimes called a 'reflective journal'. This will be part of your SOLAP (Student Officer Learning Assessment Portfolio—see Chapter 10) and will be looked at by your trainers, tutors and supervisors. The learning diary will not be of the 'Monday, 0900 to 1200—lesson burglary, v. easy' type. Rather it is a way of getting you to go round the ELC for important incidents or events. You should use it to describe what happened, analyse why things happened as they did and set down what you will do the next time you have to deal with a similar set of circumstances. Keeping a learning diary leads to several very positive outcomes; it:

- enforces the use of the ELC;
- improves the amount of learning gained;
- shows your thought processes;
- can provide evidence of competence for National Occupational Standards (NOSs).

Let's just develop those ideas a little. Some students find aspects of the ELC uncomfortable if not difficult and given the chance they won't use it. For their force and ultimately for themselves that really isn't acceptable—if you don't learn from what you have done you will carry on doing the same and never get better. Further, as we have seen, the more you do it the easier and better it gets.

The second point is a very important and interesting one. If you know that what you are writing is going to be read by someone whose opinion you care about, then you will naturally make an effort to do the best job you can. This leads to a fuller analysis of what happened and why and so maximises the learning that you take from the event. It also provides great practice for using the ELC and, of course, practice makes perfect.

Some students worry that being open and honest in their learning diary may make them open to criticism. This is to make the mistake of forgetting the first rule of experiential learning—there is no failure only feedback. By allowing your tutor to see your thought processes, you are actually providing them with a much better opportunity to help you develop. Not being honest with the people whose job it is to help you reach the required standard is a bit like lying to your doctor—ultimately self-defeating.

Finally, a well written diary entry can provide excellent evidence for some of the performance criteria in the NOSs. If you have to write a diary entry anyway, why not make it do two jobs and save yourself some effort.

Forces do seem to vary in how much emphasis they place on learning diaries, in some they are regarded as a key element of initial training and are heavily scrutinised. Regardless of the weight placed on them by the force they are an extremely useful tool for the individual officer in promoting the skills necessary for fast and easy development and learning.

11.4 **Advanced techniques**

The 'what', 'so what', 'now what' model we have used above is a very powerful tool and one that is standard across all forces. However, it is not the only way for getting experiential learning, and your goal is to develop your skills as a police officer—not simply to do what your trainers ask of you. So you might want to find out about and use some advanced techniques. One that is very simple but very effective, and superb for developing inter-personal skills, is known as the 'three position method'. Figure 11.3 will help you follow the explanation:

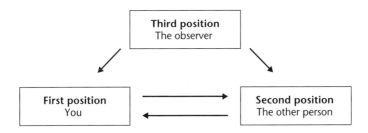

Figure 11.3 The three position method

This method is used to get the maximum learning from an interaction with someone else. A common situation where it works very well is an interview; it does not matter whether you are the interviewer or the interviewee, it works just as well for both.

So, the first step is to go back, in your mind's eye, to the start of the interview and remember how you were, mentally and physically at that time—what is known as 'going to first position'. Remember how you felt and what you were thinking. When first using this technique, it helps to actually adopt the posture and body language you used at the time. Now think about what you were trying to achieve in and from the interview and then 'run the video'; see what you saw, hear what you heard and feel how you felt. You will probably find this process happens very quickly; even a long interview can be replayed in this way in only a minute or two.

Now you need to look at the interview from the perspective of the other person, go to 'second position'. Again, until you are familiar and comfortable with the technique, it helps to actually get up and move round so you are 'facing yourself' and adopt the posture and body language of the other person. Now think about what the other person felt during the interview and how they saw you; do this as if you actually were the other person. You will probably find this an illuminating experience, but if you want to benefit from the full learning experience you need to go to the 'third position'.

So go off to one side and take a position in between the first and second positions. When you are first practising the technique you will probably find it helpful to actually get up and move to the position (if you really want to get a different perspective physically move to the position and then stand on a chair). Now put yourself in the role of an independent and impartial observer. In that role look at 'you' and the other person and consider the feelings and responses of each. Having done that tell the person at first position how they could have improved their performance and got a better result—to maintain the integrity of the exercise make sure you deliver this message in the second person, i.e. 'You should have . . .'.

Analysing an interaction using the 'three position method' is a skill, and, like any other skill, it needs practice. That said, it seldom if ever takes more than five minutes to complete and the amount of learning that can be gained, and thus the improvement of inter-personal skills, is impressive.

In this chapter we have looked at experiential learning, a key plank in modern police training. The reason it is given so much importance is that it has proved far more effective than the 'inoculation' method of training whereby people have their dose and are thereby rendered immune from any further training in that area. If ever you hear people say that they have 'had' their diversity training or 'law update training' (as though they were jabs needed before going on holiday) you'll know that they are doomed to repeat the mistakes of their past. Unlike taking antibiotics, in police training simply 'finishing the course' is not good enough.

If you do join the police you will need to become proficient at learning to do things better by analysing what you have done, and by looking on mistakes and errors as opportunities to learn—not as failures. Becoming very good at experiential learning is a skill that you will need, not only to get through the first two years, but throughout your career—as you will see in the next chapter when we examine the subject of continuous professional development.

FURTHER READING

→ <http://www.reviewing.co.uk/research/experiential.learning.htm>
This is a very good site in which the theories underpinning experiential learning are explored in layman's terms.

→ Jennifer Moon, *A Handbook of Reflective and Experiential Learning: Theory and Practice*, 2004, Routledge Falmer

12

CONTINUOUS PROFESSIONAL DEVELOPMENT

We have been talking in this part of the book about *initial* training and the question you may be asking is 'When does the training end?' The answer to that would be 'On the day you retire from the office of constable'.

12.1 **Why bother?**

We saw in Chapter 2 that society is constantly changing and so the laws that govern the way we live are similarly evolving, and new legislation that is relevant to the police is introduced all the time. As a police officer you have to keep your knowledge up to date. It is not enough to pass your exams and assessments in the first two years and then forget about it.

You know by now that when police officers exercise one of their powers, they do so under their own responsibility. So if they make, say, an arrest that turns out to be unlawful because the law had changed and they didn't know about it, it will be nobody's fault but theirs — and they could expect to receive some robust feedback through the discipline system.

In addition to new laws passed by Parliament, the Service is adopting a culture of continuous improvement; it is constantly looking for ways it can do the job faster, more efficiently and to a higher standard. This means that its own internal policies and procedures are constantly being updated (and some of these have an even bigger impact than a change in legislation); there are also new skills to learn as equipment is changed or introduced for the first time.

All forces provide on-going training, especially when a major piece of legislation is enacted, and some forces actually have a training day built into the shift pattern. However, such training cannot cover everything and what we said at the end of Chapter 11 about 'inoculations' applies every bit as much after you have finished your probation as it does during those first two years. Put simply, as a police officer you have a responsibility to keep up to date for all your service. That said, there are incentives for doing so.

Policing is, as a matter of policy and necessity, becoming more and more professional in the full sense of the word. Part of the process of turning a force of artisans into a service staffed by professionals is to ensure that the people delivering that service are competent to do so. Every officer (and indeed all other members of staff) will have a Personal Development Portfolio and be subject to an annual personal development review. They will have to be signed off by their managers as competent against the occupational standards applicable to their role—National Occupational Standards (NOSs) no longer apply only to the probationary period. Those who cannot demonstrate full competence will be given assistance to develop in their weak areas, but if that opportunity is not taken their career is likely to be very much shorter than they might have hoped. For those who are fully competent there will be a pay boost. At the moment this only applies to officers at the top of their pay scale, but within the next few years competency-related payments will almost certainly become the norm.

12.2 **Specialist posts**

Even before any changes to the pay arrangements, there are significant benefits for those that take their personal development seriously. You will be aware by now of the many roles that are open to officers within the Service and you may be aware of at least some sub-specialisms (e.g. counter-terrorist officers are selected from the ranks of CID—the Criminal Investigation Department). When it comes to filling vacancies in specialist departments those in charge of them will invariably select the candidates with the best knowledge and the most skills (anyone who isn't fully competent as a 'basic' police officer won't even be considered). The police service has a knowledge and skills economy—those who know and can do the most get the best rewards. Most forces are small enough that the reputation of a good officer will go before them, and jobs will be open to them—of course the opposite applies to those with a less than acceptable standing.

Getting selected for a specialist post will mean a new role profile and so new occupational standards to master and new legislation to learn. The most common specialism is CID and it is worth looking at what becoming a fully fledged detective entails, for it is a good illustration of the way the Service is developing and becoming more professional.

12.3 **Professionalisation of Investigations Programme and the Criminal Investigation Department**

Part of the police reform programme is aimed at:

- increasing public satisfaction with, and confidence in, the police; and
- improving the number of offenders brought to justice and therefore the proportion of crimes that are detected.

To achieve these two interlinked aims it is essential that the skills of all officers in detecting crime are improved and those new standards are maintained. With that as the objective the Service has introduced a national system for registering and accrediting investigators who have to prove their competence to the level appropriate for their role. This is the Professionalisation of Investigations Programme (PIP).

There are three levels of PIP accreditation.

- **Level 1**—aimed at all police constables, police staff and supervisors who are responsible for investigating anti-social behaviour and volume crime.

- **Level 2**—at this level are dedicated investigators, including all detective constables and sergeants, who investigate more serious and problematic crimes.

- **Level 3**—is for senior investigating officers (SIOs) who lead investigations in the case of murder, stranger-rape, kidnap or crimes of complexity. Here we are looking at detective inspectors and above.

As an officer joining the Service, your initial training will take you to Level 1 as a matter of course. To become a detective constable, the first step on the CID ladder, you will have to qualify at Level 2. There is, as you would expect, a process for doing this.

The first step is to get your application for CID endorsed by your managers and be selected for further training. This is where that good reputation as being hard working, successful, competent and knowledgeable comes in. Once you have been accepted you will have three months to study for the national CID entry examination. This is designed to test that your knowledge of law and procedure is up to the standard required of a new detective. The exam is not easy and will require a level of knowledge well above that which a street-duty officer needs; you will also have to study for it in your own time.

Once you have passed the exam you will join a CID office as a temporary detective constable. You will then have 12 months to demonstrate that you are competent against all the NOSs for your new role. In doing so you will have a portfolio similar to, but somewhat smaller than, the SOLAP you had as a student officer, and the process is very much the same. Once you have proved your competence you will become a fully fledged detective, able to begin what, for many, is the most satisfying and challenging job in the Service. You may also be eligible to apply for specialist detective posts such as fraud investigation and counter-terrorism work.

Continuous professional development is the duty of every officer, but if you embrace it fully it becomes one of the joys of being a police officer. There is always something new to learn. The study skills you developed to pass the initial training that we looked at in Chapter 10 and your ability to apply the methods of experiential learning we examined in Chapter 11 will be in constant use—and will, themselves, improve. In the next part of the book we will look at some basic law and legal concepts. This will give you a flavour for the sort of things you will have to learn and what you learn from the following chapters will stand you in good stead if you do join the Service.

FURTHER READING

→ <http://www.reviewing.co.uk/research/experiential.learning.htm>
This is a very good site in which the theories underpinning experiential learning are explored in layman's terms.

PART IV

POLICING POWERS

13

HUMAN RIGHTS AND
POLICE POWERS

If you look back to the very beginning of this book at the attestation you will be required to take on becoming a constable, you will see that a significant part of your duty in the office is to 'uphold fundamental human rights'. You may well have heard or read a lot of stories in the media over recent years about how this duty has been discharged both within the Service and by other government agencies. It has to be said that not all of those stories have been written with complete objectivity and respect for the issues in mind, and as Human Rights are a fundamental part of every officer's obligations, in this chapter we will look at what is really meant.

13.1 The European Convention on Human Rights

In the aftermath of the Second World War the countries of Western Europe decided that some guarantee was required to ensure that the horrors and abuses perpetrated by some during that conflict could never be repeated. The result was, to give it its full title, 'The European Convention for the Protection of Human Rights and Fundamental Freedoms'.

The Convention was drafted with a very large input by the British Government of the day and was signed by all the countries in the Council of Europe in 1959 as a treaty legally binding on all of them.

Thus the protection of fundamental human rights is neither new nor something that has been imposed on the UK as part of its obligations as a member of the European Union (EU). That said, all members of the EU, including those from the former communist states, have now signed the treaty.

What is much more recent is the Human Rights Act 1998. Until this piece of legislation the British Government and all its agencies were bound to uphold the human rights of its citizens, but if someone had a grievance they had to go to the European Court of Human Rights in Strasbourg to have their case heard—something very few people did. What the Act did was to integrate the Convention into UK law, thus allowing its citizens to seek redress through the UK Courts. It also—and this makes it a very significant Act, particularly for police officers—insists that all other laws must be interpreted *and applied* so as to be compliant with the Convention. Notably all laws, courts and legal proceedings in England and Wales must be compliant with people's rights under the Convention.

13.2 **Public authorities**

The aim of the Convention, and thus the Human Rights Act 1998, was to protect the individual from the State; it says nothing about relations between private individuals. So if your next-door neighbour infringes your right to a private life (we will look at our specific rights in a moment) by, for example, playing very loud music at all hours you cannot institute proceedings under the Human Rights Act, though you will certainly have other legal avenues open to you.

So what does the Act class as the State? The term used is 'public authority'. Whether a body is a public authority or not will be determined by the type of work or function that it carries out. Some are obvious, for example: government departments, local authorities, the courts, the fire and ambulance services and, of course, the police. Some may be less apparent. The companies that provide the utilities (water, gas, electricity and public transport) may not be owned by the State but they make their money by providing essential goods and services without which modern society could not function. Therefore, for the purposes of the Act they are likely to be regarded as public authorities. Other examples would include private security companies providing prisoner escort and detention services, and fully owned public bodies such as the BBC.

All public authorities, and all the people working for them, have to pay due regard to people's rights under the Convention when exercising *all and any* of their functions. It is very important that you note that not only will your force be bound by the Act but you as an individual have a duty in law as well as in the attestation to carry out your work with due regard to it.

As you read through the next few chapters, you will come across boxes in the text. You'll have seen similar ones in earlier chapters. These boxes are designed to reinforce the relevant points, to stretch your understanding and to keep you thinking about wider issues as you read. Here is an example:

ATTENTION TO DETAIL

If a person plays a noisy stereo on a train and, so infringes your right to a private life, you cannot use the European Convention against that person directly. But what about the train operating company if they failed to take action?

13.3 The Convention rights

One of the reasons that our rights and, as police officers, obligations under the Convention went without much notice for so long was that they were pretty much those freedoms which we have been fortunate enough to enjoy in the UK for a very long time. If you think about those things which make up a truly free country, the basic rights that you would want for yourself, your family and your friends, most of them are covered in the Convention. In fact some are so fundamental that we have taken them for granted for centuries—like the right to liberty and freedom of speech.

Once in the police service you will not be required to learn the Articles and Protocols of the Convention, but you will need to know what they generally say. How else can you ensure you do your duty by them? The rights and protocols are summarised below.

Obligation to respect human rights (Article 1)

This simply binds those countries which sign the Convention to abide by its terms.

Right to life (Article 2)

Everyone's right to life shall be protected by law.

Freedom from torture (Article 3)

No one shall be subjected to torture or to inhuman or degrading treatment.

Freedom from slavery and forced labour (Article 4)

No one shall be held in slavery or servitude. No one shall be required to perform forced or compulsory labour.

Right to liberty and security (Article 5)

Everyone has the right to liberty and security of person. No one shall be deprived of his/her liberty, save in accordance with a procedure prescribed by law.

Everyone who is arrested shall be informed promptly, in a language which he/she understands, of the reasons for his/her arrest and of any charge against him/her.

Everyone arrested or detained shall be brought promptly before a judge or other officer and shall be entitled to a trial within a reasonable time or to be released pending trial.

Right to a fair trial (Article 6)

In the determination of his/her civil rights and obligations or of any criminal charge against him/her, everyone is entitled to a fair and public hearing within a reasonable time by an independent and impartial tribunal established by law.

Everyone charged with a criminal offence shall be presumed innocent until proven guilty.

No punishment without crime (Article 7)

No one shall be held guilty of any criminal offence on account of any act or omission which did not constitute a criminal offence under national or international law at the time when it was committed.

Right to private life (Article 8)

Everyone has the right to respect for his/her private and family life, home and correspondence.

Freedom of thought (Article 9)

Everyone has the right to freedom of thought, conscience and religion.

Freedom of expression (Article 10)

Everyone has the right to freedom of expression.

Freedom of assembly and association (Article 11)

Everyone has the right to freedom of peaceful assembly and to freedom of association with others, including the right to form and to join trade unions for the protection of his/her interests.

Right to marry (Article 12)

Men and women of marriageable age have the right to marry, and to found a family, according to the laws of that state.

Prohibition of discrimination in Convention rights (Article 14)

The enjoyment of rights and freedoms set forth in this Convention shall be secured without discrimination on any ground such as sex, race, colour, language, religion, association with a national minority, property, birth or other status.

Protection of property (Protocol 1, Article 1)

Every natural or legal person is entitled to the peaceful protection of their possessions.

Right to education (Protocol 1, Article 2)

No person shall be denied the right to education.

Right to free elections (Protocol 1, Article 3)

The parties [to the Convention] undertake to hold free elections at reasonable intervals by secret ballot, under conditions which will ensure free expression of the opinion of the people.

There should have been no surprises; the rights are probably no more or less than you would expect.

You may have noticed the absence of an Article 13, indeed as someone who, perhaps, wants to join the Service I would hope you did—attention to detail is so important for a police officer. The reason for its absence here is that it deals with the right to an effective remedy when your other rights are breached. It is not specifically mentioned in the Human Rights Act 1998, not least because that Act in itself provides the means for the inclusion of such remedies with national law.

The rights and freedoms set out above are universal, that is they apply to everyone in England and Wales. However, if you think about them for a few minutes you will see that the exercise of one person's individual rights might well impact on the rights and freedoms of another, indeed they might be in direct conflict. These are practical issues of great importance, especially to you as a police officer, so let us give them some consideration.

13.4 **Balancing competing rights and needs**

The first thing to note is that our rights under the Convention come in two types. Some are *absolute*. That means that there is no room for debate, no watering down of their protection; infringement of them is prohibited—full stop. The right to freedom from torture (under Article 3) is an example of an absolute right. Other rights can be limited or restricted if necessary in certain circumstances in order to allow society to function. These are known as *qualified* rights. A good example would be the right to freedom of expression. Article 9 allows us to think what we like and Article 10 gives us the freedom to express those thoughts, but what if those thoughts are, for example, grossly offensive to another person? Similarly there are frequently occasions where the rights of an individual will conflict with the needs of the general public—the right to freedom of assembly against the need to allow people to go about their business, for instance. Very often the police have to balance these rights when making decisions on the streets. Sometimes this is done by senior officers (for example in allowing demonstrations to take place in certain areas) but frequently it will be down to the street-duty police officer to make a decision then and there.

The Convention recognised that there would be a need for the police, courts, local authorities and others to balance the expression or use of qualified rights and so many of its Articles include relevant limitations or exceptions. Although different ones apply to different Articles, three key features need to be considered when making decisions about balancing rights—the 'three tests'.

13.5 **The three tests**

Where the Convention gives individuals particular rights, any limitation of them will be carefully examined and must be cautiously applied. If this were not the case our rights could be overridden by any number of 'get out' clauses introduced by an unscrupulous State. Therefore, in very general terms, any limitations on rights conferred by the Convention must be:

- prescribed in law;
- intended to achieve a legitimate objective; *and*
- necessary and proportionate.

Let us look at these more closely.

Test 1: Prescribed by law

This means that there must be some clearly published law passed by the nation's normal process which allows the restriction on individuals' rights. Acts of Parliament that grant the police powers of arrest would be good examples of something that meets the first test.

Under the Human Rights Act 1998 the relevant government minister must certify that any proposed new law is compatible with our rights under the Convention. This is designed to ensure that no government is able to circumvent the Convention by simply introducing national laws which abrogate rights and freedoms conferred by it. You should note that such ministerial certificates can, and no doubt will, be challenged in the courts and the courts can and have declared that certain laws are incompatible with the Convention—forcing the Government to change them.

Such safeguards ensure that our laws are compatible with the Convention, but this still does not control the way in which such laws are *used*. An example would be police powers of arrest. The officer might have a certain power given to him or her by law in accordance with the Convention. However, the way in which he or she uses that power is also of critical importance; hence the reason for test 2.

Test 2: Intended to achieve a legitimate objective

The purpose of this test is to ensure that the powers that are prescribed by laws satisfying test 1 are being *used* for the right reason. This second test ensures that, for example, just because the police have the power to arrest people and search their property, such powers are used only when in the proper discharge of their duties. Another example would be the misuse of official data. As a police officer you are entitled to view information on the owners of motor cars, but only as is necessary for you to do your job—looking up the details of a car you were thinking of buying would be a breach of the Convention. This second test is still not sufficient to ensure that individual rights and freedoms are properly protected, so we have the further safety net of test 3.

Test 3: Necessary and proportionate

Any actions that interfere with an individual's rights under the Convention must be 'Necessary and proportionate to the end that is to be achieved'. Even though you may have a legal power granted by an Act of Parliament that passes test 1 and you use it to achieve a legitimate objective (passing test 2), your behaviour must not be over the top and heavy-handed. To satisfy test 3 you will need to be able to show that when you exercised that power it was *necessary* to do so and you were not doing more than you needed to. We will come back to the necessity test when we look at powers of arrest in the next chapter.

ATTENTION TO DETAIL

Your car is seen speeding by a speed camera on the motorway. In these circumstances the police have the power to ask you who was driving it at the time. The police also have powers to enter people's property and to carry firearms. Although these powers all come from Acts of Parliament (meeting test 1) and prosecuting speeding motorists is a legitimate objective (meeting test 2), are the police entitled to send a firearms team crashing through the windows of your house to find out who was driving your car when it was caught by the camera?

The important things to remember from this chapter are:

- Is there a public authority involved? Don't forget that the courts are public authorities so even in private disputes, such as between neighbours, any relevant rights under the Convention will need to be considered. As a police officer you have a positive duty to ensure rights are upheld, as will all your colleagues in the wider police family.

- Some rights under the Convention are limited in some way—if in doubt, check the wording of the individual Article.

- If you are thinking about any interference with a right under the Convention, apply the three tests to see how a court may look at the situation.

- Human rights is not an area of law that exists on its own—it touches every aspect of law, whether that be police powers, the laws of evidence or the wording of criminal offences themselves.

As you look at police law and procedure in the remainder of this book, and especially when you go on to study them in your training, keep these principles in mind—it's surprising where they crop up.

FURTHER READING

→ <http://www.opsi.gov.uk>

The Office of Public Sector Information is a site well worth becoming familiar with. Using its search function will give you access to all sorts of useful information including all the Acts of Parliament.

14

POWERS OF ARREST

As you saw in Part I, police officers and their colleagues are entrusted with many powers and privileges over and above those granted to their fellow citizens. The most important of these powers, both practically and constitutionally, are those that enable them to deprive their fellow citizens of their liberty and to take possession of their property—powers of arrest, search and seizure.

You may well have seen TV programmes in which police officers talk about getting warrants to arrest suspects, and news programmes frequently mention the process. However, in reality, in England and Wales police powers of arrest are extensive and it is rare for an arrest warrant to be needed. Nonetheless the existence of warrants is an important point, for all police powers can be divided into two categories—those which need the authorisation of a court (i.e. require a warrant) and those which the officer can execute without seeking authority.

Regardless of which type we are talking about, it is absolutely essential that all police officers use their powers wisely, fairly and properly. Not only must they keep in mind the Human Rights issues we looked at in Chapter 13 (especially test 3), but they must also remember that improper use of powers can lead to individual officers being liable in both the civil and criminal courts and under internal disciplinary procedures. It can also lead to evidence being inadmissible and the criminal being allowed to get away with their crime. Perhaps even more importantly, the way officers use their powers does have a direct effect on the confidence that the community has in the police.

Even when police officers exercise their powers lawfully, their actions can be perceived as a source of oppression and discrimination, leading to a lack of confidence and the creation of an atmosphere of distrust. A stark example of this would be Operation Swamp in South London in 1981. We mentioned this briefly in Part I, but just to remind you: in an attempt to reduce the incidence of street robbery an operation was mounted in which great use was made of the existing powers to stop and search. Those powers were lawful and they were used to a legitimate end, but the perception amongst a sufficiently large section of the community was such that the worst riots for, probably, a century broke out and the relationship between the police and the community was changed forever.

If you ask anyone who is not a police officer, or who has not read this book, what powers the police have that their fellow citizens don't, they will probably name the power of arrest first. Powers of arrest are probably the most widely known—and the most widely misunderstood. When you come to study them closely you will see that in many situations anyone has the power to arrest suspects, not just police officers. However, police officers do have specific powers to arrest and detain that are much wider than other citizens and it is only with those that we will concern ourselves in this chapter.

So what is an 'arrest'? If you were forced to come up with a definition you might say that it was taking someone to a police station against their will, and that wouldn't be a bad summary. An arrest generally involves stopping someone from going where they please, by force if *necessary*—you don't need to take them anywhere—in connection with an allegation of a criminal offence that has, or is suspected of having, taken place (we will look at what we mean by criminal offence in Chapter 16).

In modern times, since the late 1960s, a distinction in law has been made between *arrest* and *detention.* The police have many powers to detain people short of arresting them. When you stop a motorist whilst controlling traffic you are, in effect, stopping them going about their business in a way that they may wish; but generally speaking the use of the word *detention* is reserved for more formal occasions. An example would be to detain someone for the purpose of a search (we will look at this in the next chapter) or, under the Football (Disorder) Act 2000, a police officer may detain someone who has been banned from attending matches so as to stop them from travelling to a game. Additionally some of the wider police family have powers to detain people under certain circumstances — such as police community support officers who may, in defined situations, detain a member of the public until a constable arrives on the scene. It is important to keep the issues of arrest and detention as separate in your mind as they are in law, not least because, as any police officer will tell you, with an arrest comes a whole host of responsibilities and powers that do not follow if someone has merely been detained.

So, although arrests are usually made in connection with a criminal offence that has already taken place, occasionally they may be made for other reasons such as:

- to *prevent* something taking place (such as a breach of the peace);
- to take DNA samples or fingerprints;
- to return someone to prison who is unlawfully at large or to bring them before a court.

Usually a person is arrested because the officer suspects that they have done something wrong. However, there are also occasions when someone maybe arrested because they:

- are about to do something wrong;
- might do something wrong unless they are arrested;
- have *not* done something that they were lawfully required to do (for example a motorist who failed to provide a breath test when lawfully required to do so).

It is very important that you realise that, although an officer may have the power to arrest someone, it does not mean he or she has to. We will come back to this point later but for now remember two things:

1. There is no general duty to arrest even when there is a power to do so; alternatives should always be considered.

2. An arrest is an exercise of personal responsibility. It is your power, your decision and you will have to be able to justify what you did—possibly in front of a judge. Nobody can order you to make an arrest except a court.

ATTENTION TO DETAIL

You may have noticed that an arrest is an interference with a person's rights under the European Convention to liberty and freedom of movement. Therefore, aside from all other considerations, the three tests (especially the third) will apply to the use of any power to arrest by the police or any other public authority.

14.1 **Lawful arrests**

Every arrest must be lawful—otherwise it is unlawful. This may sound like a very obvious statement, but it is extremely important. The person carrying out the arrest—like anyone using any legal power—*must* be able to point to some legal authority which allows them to do it. When you bring your prisoner before the custody officer you are going to have to justify your actions then and there. You will have to say why and for what offence you have arrested the person, and from that will be judged whether or not you had a power and why the arrest was necessary. Leaving the last point aside for a moment (we will come back to it in some detail in the section below), the power to arrest may come from the following sources:

- the circumstances at the time;
- the provisions of a particular Act;
- an order of a court.

The last of these three you can note and then, for now, forget about. Powers that come from a court are easy to deal with; the court issues a warrant telling you who to arrest and you do it. The police powers that you need to worry about are those granted by various Acts of Parliament that you can exercise without reference to anybody else. These are described as powers of arrest *without warrant*.

Most (but by no means all) police powers of arrest, search and seizure come from one particular Act—the Police and Criminal Evidence Act 1984, more commonly known, as we saw in Chapter 2, as PACE. Although it was passed more than 20 years ago, PACE has been regularly amended and updated, particularly by the Serious Organised Crime and Police Act 2005 (SOCPA). What follows relates to the powers of *police officers* to arrest without warrant.

14.2 **The power to arrest**

Until January of 2006 the powers of arrest without warrant for a constable were complex. The offence in question had to be sufficiently serious that the offender could receive five years in gaol, or Parliament would specifically have had to have given a power of arrest or certain general conditions would have had to have been met. Since then, the provisions of section 110 of the SOCPA have been introduced and life at first sight is much simpler.

The effect of this section is to modernise the powers of arrest for police officers and ordinary citizens. The latter need not concern us here; we need only concern ourselves with what a constable can do. This is contained in section 24 of PACE and appears to be quite straightforward—let us look at what it actually says.

Section 24   Arrest without warrant: constables

(1) A constable may arrest without a warrant—
- (a) anyone who is about to commit an offence;
- (b) anyone who is in the act of committing an offence;
- (c) anyone whom he has reasonable grounds for suspecting to be about to commit an offence;
- (d) anyone whom he has reasonable grounds for suspecting to be committing an offence.

(2) If a constable has reasonable grounds for suspecting that an offence has been committed, he may arrest without a warrant anyone whom he has reasonable grounds to suspect of being guilty of it.

(3) If an offence has been committed, a constable may arrest without a warrant—
- (a) anyone who is guilty of the offence;
- (b) anyone whom he has reasonable grounds for suspecting to be guilty of it.

Got that? As a constable, you may now arrest anyone who you reasonably suspect (and we will look at the meaning of that phrase in a minute) is about to commit or is committing or has committed *any* offence. Yes, that's right, *any* offence; from dropping litter to murder, and even failing to ensure a child is wearing a seat belt in the back seat of a car.

At this point you may be asking yourself about the provisions of the Human Rights Act and, in particular, you may be thinking about number 3 of our three tests. If so, well done, because section 24 continues thus:

(4) But the power of summary arrest conferred by subsection (1), (2) or (3) is exercisable only if the constable has reasonable grounds for believing that for any of the reasons mentioned in subsection (5) it is necessary to arrest the person in question.

(5) The reasons are—
- (a) to enable the name of the person in question to be ascertained (in the case where the constable does not know, and

cannot readily ascertain, the person's name, or has reasonable grounds for doubting whether a name given by the person as his name is his real name);

(b) correspondingly as regards the person's address;

(c) to prevent the person in question—
  (i)   causing physical injury to himself or any other person;
  (ii) suffering physical injury;
  (iii) causing loss of or damage to property;
  (iv) committing an offence against public decency (subject to subsection (6)); or
  (v)   causing an unlawful obstruction of the highway;

(d) to protect a child or other vulnerable person from the person in question;

(e) to allow the prompt and effective investigation of the offence or of the conduct of the person in question;

(f) to prevent any prosecution for the offence from being hindered by the disappearance of the person in question.

(6) Subsection (5)(c)(iv) applies only where members of the public going about their normal business cannot reasonably be expected to avoid the person in question.

This is the 'necessity test' which keeps police powers of arrest in line with the European Convention on Human Rights. In short what the law says is that a police officer can now arrest anybody on reasonable suspicion that they are about to commit, are committing or have committed any offence as long as it is *necessary* to do so (remember test 3 of the 'three tests' in the previous chapter).

Parliament has done its best to set down what circumstances will and will not be accepted as making an arrest necessary, and they probably look fairly straightforward to you, but you can be sure that there will be an awful lot of cases regarding this coming before the higher courts over the next few years.

A couple of things are definitely worthy of note here. Firstly, the guidance issued by the Home Office to accompany the introduction of the new powers is quite specific. It states that an arrest must never be made just because it can be and officers must consider the use of alternatives (e.g. reporting for summons or a fixed penalty notice). The guidance also states that the officer should take into account the situation of the victim, the nature of the offence, the circumstances of the offender and the needs of the investigation when deciding whether to arrest. You may, by now, be seeing just how close the necessity test is to the third of the three tests we looked at when we considered the Human Rights Act.

The second thing to note is use of the term 'reasonable belief' for the necessity test and 'reasonable suspicion' for the power to arrest itself. In law, belief and suspicion are not synonymous. There is a difference in the degree of certainty required for each. Suspicion has been held to be a 'State of conjecture where proof is lacking'. On the other hand, belief implies that there is more information available that turns the conjecture into an acceptance that something is true. If you like to think of it in this way: if there are ten steps between pure conjecture and absolute certainty then reasonable suspicion is at step two or three; reasonable belief, however, is at step eight or nine.

Whether, as an officer, you had reasonable suspicion or belief is always a matter for the courts to decide. The key word is reasonable. You must always be able to state the facts and information that you had at the time and why they gave rise to the suspicion or belief on which you based your decision. The court will decide whether, on the facts as given and in the circumstances of the case, an ordinary person *could* have come to the same conclusions as the officer. Again this illustrates the fact that a police officer must always be prepared to justify their decisions based on fact and law. When you can't it gets very, very lonely standing in the witness box before a judge and jury, to say nothing of the possible consequences later.

Finally, just look at the first reasons of the necessity test again. Generally speaking it is not an offence for a person to fail to give their name and address to a constable (there are exceptions—the main one being the drivers of motor cars on the public highway). However, as you can see, if a person reasonably suspected of any offence fails to give his or her details (or gives such that the officer may reasonably believe them to be false) it does make them liable to arrest *for the offence* regardless of any other consideration.

ATTENTION TO DETAIL

You may wonder what happens if, having had the chance to re-think the wisdom of using Mickey Mouse's name, the arrested person decides to give their real name and address on the way to the police station.

Well, if the grounds for making the arrest come to an end before they reach the station, and providing there are no further grounds for detaining them, the officer *must* release the person.

One last point before leaving this subject — if the officer already knows the person's name and address, they could only arrest if they had grounds under one of the other conditions.

14.3 **Tell them what is happening**

Whenever a person is arrested and for whatever reason, the law (PACE) makes it very clear that the person must be told that they are under arrest and why — even if it should be obvious to them. The only exception is where the person escapes before the officer could give them the information. Even when the person is violent or drunk, they must be told that they are being arrested and why as soon as practicable.

Although these requirements come from PACE, you'll probably remember Article 5 of the European Convention on Human Rights, which says that:

Everyone who is arrested shall be informed promptly, in a language that he/she understands, of the reason for his/her arrest and any charge against him/her.

So it is an added requirement to make sure that the arrested person is given the information in a language that they understand. This is particularly important if you have arrested someone whose first language is not English or who has a serious hearing impairment (in which case you'll need to get hold of a competent signer as soon as possible after the arrest). The other thing you have to tell people when they are arrested, or about to be questioned about an offence, is the caution.

14.4 **A word of caution**

Almost every American TV cop show ends with the villain being 'read his rights'—the part where usually the hero's sidekick gets out a little card and says 'You have the right to remain silent'. Well, in England and Wales we have to do something similar.

ATTENTION TO DETAIL

The more compulsive movie and TV addicts will know that the process in the United States is called the *Miranda* process. This comes from the case where the US Supreme Court decided that all suspects must be told of their rights when arrested (*Miranda v The State of Arizona*). By this stage you should be able to guess where the English and Welsh equivalent comes from—PACE.

Before worrying about the exact wording of the caution, you should note that it is the principle behind it that is the most important thing. The idea is to alert the person who is being arrested, or is to be questioned, of their right not to say anything and to warn them that anything they say may be used in evidence against them in court. It is also a warning that by not saying anything they may be harming any defence which they later use in court. The actual wording of the caution has been designed to get this message across in the simplest way possible and it has been carefully written to make it as easy as possible for everyone.

The law does allow some minor variations in the words that are actually used. However, if you use different words you may, unwittingly, give a different meaning. Not only would that be unfair on the person under arrest, it could also jeopardise the whole case. So it is better just to memorise the caution and use the exact words every time. It goes like this:

> *You do not have to say anything. But it may harm your defence if you do not mention when questioned something which you later rely on in court. Anything you do say may be given in evidence.*

It is only 37 words in the 3 short sentences. If you are going to join the police you may as well start learning the caution now.

Generally speaking, under PACE a person must be cautioned when they are arrested and before each time they are questioned about their involvement in a criminal offence.

ATTENTION TO DETAIL

You won't be surprised to learn that not everyone 'comes quietly' when they are arrested. You may wonder what happens when the officer is unable to get through the 37 words when wrestling with a violent drunk. Thankfully the law and common sense coincide. PACE states that you do not have to administer the caution where the behaviour or the condition of the arrested person makes it impracticable to do so. Note that this is slightly different from the requirement to tell people they are under arrest and why (see above).

PACE goes on to provide that, if a person does not appear to understand what the caution means, the officer who has given it should go on to explain it in his or her own words. This is important, not only when dealing with someone whose first language is not English (in which case you should always think about getting an interpreter), but also when there is some doubt as to the person's ability to understand what is going on. If in doubt, err on the side of 'caution'!

One last thing before leaving the subject of the caution, always make an accurate note of exactly what the person says after you have cautioned them, and make sure you include it, word for word, in your evidence. Not only will people often make highly revealing statements in the heat of the moment, sometimes they will say something that later provides the key to the whole case. They can also say stupid and insulting things, but whatever they say make sure you make a note of it and put it in your statement; there is no need to feel embarrassed by someone else's ignorance or stupidity.

EXAMPLE

Many years ago at a city magistrates' court one of the 'regular custom-ers' was an unlicensed street trader who used to get himself arrested two or three times a month. Every time after he was cautioned he replied, 'It's a fair cop, guv, but society is to blame'. This was so regular that the magistrates used to listen out for it and woe betide the arresting officer who, out of embarrassment or some other reason—fear of not being believed mainly—did not have it in his or her evidence.

14.5 A word about force

The law allows the use of such force as is *reasonable* when making an arrest. Whether any force used was reasonable will be decided by the court in the light of all the circumstances, including the situation as the officer believed it to be at the time. On some very rare occasions the force used by an officer may even be lethal to the other person. Police officers are given expert training in proper ways to respond and behave in situations where violence may be anticipated.

Police powers of arrest have been greatly simplified; now a constable can arrest if he or she reasonably suspects a person is about to commit or is committing or has committed *any* offence *providing* he or she reasonably believes it is necessary to do so. We have seen that there is a significant difference between what you need for suspicion and what you need for belief.

In the next four chapters we start looking at what actually makes up a criminal offence.

FURTHER READING

→ <http://www.blackstonespolicemanuals.com>
   Blackstone's are the main publishers of the standard police textbooks.

→ <http://www.opsi.gov.uk>

→ Brian Fitzpatrick, *Going to Court*, 2006, Oxford University Press

15

STOP AND SEARCH

In addition to their powers of arrest, another important power given to the police is the power to stop and search people and vehicles. This is probably the most controversial of police powers and it is essential that all officers have a full understanding, not only of what powers they have, but when, where and how they should be used. We have already mentioned in previous chapters what can happen when officers use powers to stop and search insensitively; remember Operation Swamp that led to the Brixton riots.

By this time there is probably no need to say where the powers come from—it is the Police and Criminal Evidence Act 1984 (PACE). PACE also has Codes of Practice to help people interpret its provisions and set guidelines to be followed. These Codes must be made available in every police station, and a breach of them by an officer will almost certainly amount to a disciplinary offence. The relevant Code of Practice setting out how stop and search powers should be used are in Code A.

15.1 Where?

Generally, a police officer may use the power to stop and search in public places. This will include places that are open to the public on payment (for example museums, cinemas and sports stadiums). It does not include people's homes or any attached land. However, if a person that an officer wishes to search is in a garden which is part of a house, the power to search may be used provided that the officer has '*reasonable grounds for believing*' that the person does not live there *and* that they are not in the garden with the permission of someone who does live there. If you think about it this makes sense; whilst it would be unreasonable to routinely search people in their own gardens, it is necessary for the police to have a power to stop and search people who are in someone else's garden—as burglars often are! This is another example where Parliament and the police have to balance people's competing human rights.

These restrictions relate to where the person to be searched must have been found. You do not have to carry out the search in the same place. In fact for some searches the person should be taken out of public view. You need to be careful how you do this, for, whilst the intention is to spare the person embarrassment, it can be seen as sinister or excessive.

15.2 **What?**

You may search any person, any vehicle and anything that is in or on the vehicle (luggage, roof boxes, tool kits etc.). You may search for stolen or prohibited articles, the latter generally being weapons or tools for use in the course of a crime. The power to search includes a power to detain the person for '*as long as is reasonably necessary*' for the search to be carried out.

ATTENTION TO DETAIL

So far in this chapter we have seen 'reasonable grounds for believing' and 'as long as is reasonably necessary'; soon we will meet 'reasonable grounds for suspecting'. As with arrests, what is reasonable will be a matter for the courts, and the officer will have to be able to say what facts and information caused him or her to have the belief or suspicion (which carry the same meanings here as we saw in the last chapter).

15.3 **When?**

Before an officer can use their power to stop and search someone they must have 'reasonable grounds for suspecting' that, as a result of the search, they will find stolen or prohibited articles. Whether as the police officer you would have such reasonable grounds must be decided in the light of all the circumstances at the time. Usually it will be the behaviour of the person, perhaps combined with the location and time of day, or possibly information that you have received from a third party which will enable you to decide whether there are such reasonable grounds. As always you will have to be able to justify your decision after the event.

Once you have a reasonable suspicion then, and only then, can you stop someone in order to search them. It isn't lawful for you to go on 'fishing expeditions' where you stop people with the intention of finding grounds to afford suspicion that they are carrying stolen or prohibited articles. Nor can you continue if you know that there is no likelihood of finding the articles (perhaps because you saw the person throw them into the canal or give them to someone else). What you should do in such circumstances is beyond the scope of this book; suffice it to say that it will be covered in depth during initial training.

Reasonable suspicion can never be founded on the basis of purely personal factors such as a person's race, colour, age or hairstyle. The unacceptability of stereotyping people on the appearance or perceived membership of a particular group is discussed elsewhere in this book. As well as it being a breach of their duty to respect race and diversity, the fact that police officers must not stop and search on the basis of personal features alone is also made quite clear in Code A of the PACE Codes of Practice.

Nevertheless, Code A does allow for the searching of members of gangs or groups who are known to habitually carry:

- knives unlawfully, or
- weapons, or
- controlled drugs

and who wear distinctive items of clothing or other things to identify themselves with such a group or gang.

15.4 **How?**

This is very important. Code A sets out how any search must be carried out. The cooperation of the person must be sought in every case and, although force could ultimately be used, this should be viewed very much as a last resort. Indeed, if a person is unwilling to cooperate or actually physically resists being searched then it is probably time to move to an arrest rather than try to persevere with a search.

Having stopped a person to search them, there is *no requirement* to do so. It may turn out from a moment's conversation that a search is either not required or it is impracticable to carry out.

ATTENTION TO DETAIL

One oddity about the power to stop and search under PACE is that it doesn't authorise the officer to stop a vehicle. It authorises the searching of a vehicle, as we have seen, and anything carried in or on it, but the Act is silent on how the constable gets the vehicle to stop so that it can be searched.

In practice the problem is resolved by using the powers to stop and direct traffic under the Road Traffic Act 1988, for which the officer has to be in uniform.

If, in the course of the search, the officer finds stolen or prohibited articles he or she may seize them. The possession of such articles is almost certainly sufficient to afford reasonable suspicion that the person has committed an offence and therefore they must be cautioned (as described in Chapter 14) before any questions relating to the articles are put to them.

An officer carrying out a search must provide their name and the police station to which they are attached to the person who is to be searched. If the officer is not in uniform they must also show the person their warrant card. They must also tell the person the purpose of the search and the grounds for it.

Generally when carrying out a search an officer cannot require the person to remove any clothing in public other than their outer coat, jacket and gloves. If for the purposes of the search it is necessary to go further than this (perhaps because the items being sought are very small, e.g. stolen jewellery) then the person should be taken to a suitable private place, normally the nearest police station.

For each search and, generally speaking, at the time of the search, the officer must complete a search record. This is a small self-duplicating form that officers carry around with them. On the form are recorded the:

- name of the person searched, if they are willing to provide it—they are not obliged to—otherwise their description;
- date, time and location of the search;
- result of the search;
- grounds for the search.

The officer has to record there and then on the form the reasons why they stopped and searched the person. The subject of the search is entitled to a copy of the search record; this can be given at the time if they want it, or they can get a copy from the officer's station at a later date, up to a year after the search.

The ability to stop and search people is a valuable tool in tackling certain types of crime. However, as noted, it is a controversial power which must be used properly and with great sensitivity and discretion.

In this section we have only looked at the power to stop and search under section 1 of PACE. Police officers have other powers to search both persons and premises granted by other sections of PACE (e.g. searching after an arrest) and by other Acts of Parliament such as the Terrorism Act 2000. Whatever power is being used nobody likes having a stranger go through their possessions and far less searching their person. So the rule about sensitivity applies equally to all searches.

15.5 **Powers of entry**

If you enter someone else's property without their permission or some other legal authority you are a trespasser. This is a simple but important concept which we will come across later when we look at the offence of burglary. Although trespassing in this way isn't generally a criminal offence, it does mean that the owner can ask you to leave—and throw you out by force if you don't go! This general rule applies as much to police officers as to anyone else. So if you want to go onto someone else's property you must either:

- be invited, or
- have a legal power of entry.

In some cases the owner of the property is assumed to have given general permission for restricted access to their property. Such general permission usually applies to people having lawful business at the house to walk up the path to the front door. Again such general permissions apply to police officers in the same way as everyone else. It is important to note that if someone goes beyond the limits of the permission, by walking round to the back door for instance, or roaming around the garden or failing to leave when asked, they again become trespassers.

The difficulty comes when not only does the owner not give permission, but actively wants to stop you from entering their property.

In such cases if you do not have a legal power to go in you can't. Therefore, to enable the police to go into buildings to arrest people, to protect people, to search for things and to seize evidence, Parliament has balanced the human rights of the property owner with the needs of society and given limited powers to the police to enter property.

PACE, including Code B of the Codes of Practice, covers entry, search and seizure both with and without a warrant. Strangely enough, premises in this context also usually include boats, caravans and cars. As with other powers, these represent an interference with the private lives and property of individuals, and, therefore, must be used appropriately and only when necessary (keep remembering the Human Rights Act 1998 and the three tests).

15.6 **Powers without warrant**

Police officers still retain a common law power of entry to prevent a breach of the peace (see Chapter 16). This power is only available when officers have a genuine and reasonable belief that a breach of the peace is happening or is about to happen in the immediate future; the sound of screaming and shouting and/or furniture and fittings being thrown around would be enough. All other common law powers of entry were abolished by PACE. In their place the Act introduced wide powers of entry, search and seizure, particularly when made in connection with an arrest.

There are many Acts of Parliament that give the police (and other agencies) powers to apply to the courts for warrants authorising entry. There are also many other Acts which give the police powers of entry without a warrant. Examples of such powers are those that allow the police to enter:

- any place for the purpose of carrying out a search under the Firearms Act 1968;

- school premises in connection with weapons;
- relevant premises in connection with a police direction to leave and remove vehicles.

Of course, as we have seen, not everything a police officer does is related to crime and criminals. One occasion when an officer may need to get into a property quickly and without having to waste time seeking permission is when there is a fire inside. The specific right of a constable to enter or break into any premises or place to deal with a fire under the Fire Services Act 1947 was lost when that Act was repealed in 2004 and its successor did not replicate the old power. However, under section 17(1)(e) of PACE a constable may enter and search any premises for the purpose of saving life or preventing serious damage to property.

In this chapter we first saw that when a police officer reasonably suspects a person is carrying stolen or prohibited articles they may stop and detain them in order to search them for those articles. We then saw that the police do have some powers (mostly under PACE) to enter private property, regardless of the owner's consent. In order to be lawful these powers may only be used when they are necessary and proportionate to the task in hand, and in any case need to be used with sensitivity and discretion.

This chapter and the previous one have been about the two most important police powers, particularly when it comes to tackling crime. In the next chapter we explore what a crime actually is.

FURTHER READING

→ <http://www.blackstonespolice.com>
  Blackstone's are the main publishers of the standard police textbooks.

→ <http://www.opsi.gov.uk>

16

LAW AND ORDER

By any standards police duty is pretty unusual, if not unique. The motivation required to do it, along with the training and experience it gives you, and the level of personal responsibility it demands, makes policing very different from most other occupations. As well as the obvious commitment, energy and resilience, a sense of compassion and certainly humour, policing requires legal powers. We have already looked at some of those powers in the last two chapters.

Frequently, the role of the police in England and Wales is described as keeping law and order, but, as you have seen, the role is in fact much wider and far more complex than that. In this chapter we look at some of the key concepts in criminal law and then go on to consider some specific aspects of the law relevant to policing that are mainly concerned with keeping our communities safe.

16.1 **The law**

The first thing to note is that policing is not just about criminal law. The wide range of an officer's duties means that he or she will inevitably become involved in, and need to know about, many different areas of law. If you look back at Part II you can see that areas such as road traffic law, family law, the law relating to children, and sudden death are all part of an officer's day-to-day work. In addition the law relating to the sale of alcohol, to betting, animals, trade disputes and employment law

169

are also sometimes relevant. However, when all is said and done the main areas of law that concern police officers *are* found in the criminal law and the law relating to evidence and procedure.

When looking at criminal offences it is important to note that each one can be broken down into key elements or ingredients. In police parlance these are known as 'points to prove' because *all* of them have to be proved in evidence before a person can be convicted of the offence. If you can't obtain the evidence to show all the elements, the person cannot have committed that particular offence. They may well have committed a different offence though. An important part of an officer's skill set is to be able to recognise all the different offences that can arise out of the same set of facts and the points to prove for each, not least because if you don't know the points to prove you can't even begin looking for the evidence that you need.

The rest of this book is simply an introduction to some of the main offences that you will deal with as a street-duty police officer and a look at the basic concepts in the area. If you do join the police service it will help you get a running start to your training, where these subjects will be covered in greater detail. If you have already studied law, perhaps at school or university or in a previous job, it will act as a timely refresher.

ATTENTION TO DETAIL

It was said above that 'If you can't obtain the evidence to show all the elements, the person cannot have committed that particular offence'. This is not strictly true. The person may well have committed the offence, but without all the ingredients you will not be able to prove it in a court. Did you pick the point up? Aside from all the other qualities we have mentioned a good police officer needs an eye for legal detail.

So, police officers need to know the points to prove of all the common offences—such as theft, burglary, deception and assaults—and also be able to knowledgeably consider where some crimes overlap. They also need to understand the range of measures that have been set down by Parliament to help tackle disorder and to create community environments where people not only are safe, but *feel* safe too. An example would be applying to the courts for anti-social behaviour orders (ASBOs) where a person's behaviour is becoming a nuisance to their neighbours.

Naturally, a great deal of an officer's training is spent learning the law and powers that the police have been given to tackle crime, maintain the peace and protect life and property, as well as how and when to use those powers. The use of discretion is very important when deciding to use any police powers. You must also always remember the principles of human rights that we discussed in Chapter 13, particularly the third of the three tests.

16.2 It's a crime

What actually is a crime? Well, the classification of some unlawful behaviour into 'crimes' is actually an administrative convenience. It is used by the Government, the police and other agencies to measure and monitor criminal activity. In law there are civil torts, misdeeds that are fought over between the parties in the civil courts, and criminal offences, which are dealt with by the magistrates' and Crown Courts. Criminal offences are usually prosecuted by the State (always referred to as 'the Crown' — as in the Crown Prosecution Service), as opposed to the injured party, and result in the guilty person receiving a punishment. Civil courts can award damages, or an order forbidding or requiring a course of conduct, but do not 'punish' the guilty party in a tort case.

Some criminal offences are clearly more serious than others. For instance, having the wrong sized letters on your car's number plate is a criminal offence (you can be punished in the magistrates' court) and so is death by dangerous driving, but the two are totally different in terms of their consequences — both to the offender and the victim.

That doesn't mean that certain crimes are minor or trivial (if you want to know what crimes are 'minor' ask the victim—the answer will almost certainly be 'none'). However, the law has to treat some criminal offences as being of more significance than others. As a result some offences carry a greater maximum penalty than others. For these reasons the law divides criminal offences into 'summary offences' and 'indictable offences'.

16.3 **Summary offences**

Summary offences include almost all road traffic offences such as speeding and careless driving. However, just because an offence is classified as summary that does not mean that it is less than significant. The list of summary offences includes some offences relating to public disorder and anti-social behaviour, drunkenness and taking a vehicle without the owner's consent. These are common offences that can frequently have a significant impact on the quality of people's lives, and some are in themselves substantial offences that can attract prison sentences.

Summary offences have to be tried in the magistrates' court, either by a district judge (a qualified and experienced lawyer) or by a bench of lay magistrates—people from the local community appointed as justices of the peace. Both lay magistrates and district judges have the power to fine those found guilty or, where the offence allows, send them to prison for up to six months. The overwhelming majority of criminal cases (about 95 per cent according to recent figures) are dealt with in the magistrates' courts.

16.4 **Indictable offences**

Indictable offences are those which have more serious consequences for the victims and the community, not to mention any person that is found guilty of them. Examples would be rape, robbery, the more serious assaults, some burglaries and, of course, murder. They are called indictable because they are tried on indictment, that is to say in the Crown Court before a judge and, in most cases, a jury.

The judge in the Crown Court will be an experienced lawyer with many years' experience of criminal practice. He or she is there to preside over the trial and to decide on matters of law (such as whether a defence applied in a particular case). The jury is made up of 12 members of the community chosen, as far as practicable, by chance. Their job is to decide on questions of fact—such as whether the defendant is guilty! Generally speaking, individual jurors only ever sit on one case in their entire lives.

If, having heard all the evidence that the judge allows, the jury decides that the defendant is guilty, the judge will pass sentence. Though there are guidelines, judges have very wide discretion when it comes to punishment. The fact that an offence carries a maximum prison sentence of many years (theft for example has a maximum penalty of seven years' imprisonment) does not mean that the guilty party will receive anything like that amount or even be sent to prison at all. The only exception to this is the offence of murder where a life sentence is mandatory, though even then the judge has considerable latitude in deciding how long the person must serve before being considered for parole. Incidentally, when it comes to the investigation of crime, police officers have additional powers available to them when enquiring into indictable offences.

16.5 Either-way offences

The fact that criminal offences are divided into summary and indictable does not mean that every offence falls into one or other of those categories; very little in English and Welsh law is that straightforward.

There is in fact a third category; offences that can be tried in either the magistrates' court or the Crown Court—the choice is usually the defendant's (though the magistrates can refuse to hear it if they think their powers of sentence insufficient for the circumstances of the crime in question). Such offences are known as 'either-way offences'. These include theft, handling stolen goods, criminal deceptions, some assaults and drug offences.

16.6 **Some figures**

To help put the above discussion into context some figures may be useful. A few years ago the Government under took a major review of the work of the criminal courts in England and Wales, and you may find some of its findings both interesting and instructive (all figures relate to 1999, and can be found in 'A Review of the Criminal Courts of England and Wales by The Right Honourable Lord Justice Auld' available at <http://www.criminal-courts-review.org.uk/>).

Let us look at the number of cases of each type and the outcomes.

Summary cases dealt with in the magistrates' courts

Defendants dealt with	Found not guilty	Convicted
1,088,000	24,000	1,064,000

What is really significant about these figures is the proportion of convictions—nearly 98 per cent—of whom it must be said probably slightly more than half (firm figures are not available) pleaded guilty at the outset.

Either-way offences dealt with in the magistrates' courts

Defendants dealt with	Found not guilty	Convicted
296,000	11,000	285,000

Again a very high conviction rate (96 per cent).

Either-way offences dealt with in the Crown Courts

Defendants dealt with	Found not guilty	Convicted
56,000	13,000	43,000

Now the conviction rate drops substantially, to 77 per cent. A cynic might start to see why some defendants prefer to be tried by a jury than in the magistrates' courts; where the district judges and magistrates hear similar cases time after time, year in year out. However, only about 4 per cent of the total number of people charged with either-way offences actually elected to be tried in the Crown Court.

Indictable offences dealt with in the Crown Courts

Defendants dealt with	Found not guilty	Convicted
17,000	5,000	12,000

A conviction rate of 71 per cent. However, of those that actually pleaded not guilty (8,160) only 62 per cent were convicted.

Although these figures are now quite old (more recent ones are not easily available), evidence suggests that, while the overall numbers may be higher, the proportions of people convicted remain pretty stable year on year. Given that the overall conviction rate is approximately 96 per cent, the police do manage to obtain a conviction on a high proportion of the crimes that they detect; but some might say the problem is they don't detect enough!

16.7 **Order**

Think back to Part I and you may remember that the prime duty of the police is to keep the peace and protect life and property. This has remained unchanged since the first 'modern' police force was formed in 1829.

The police have a number of legal powers to help them maintain order. The oldest of these comes from the idea of a 'breach of the peace'. Generally speaking a breach of the peace occurs when a person is harmed, or they or their property are threatened by some form of disturbance. In such situations, as we saw in Chapter 15, the police have the power to enter premises and to detain anyone that is causing the disturbance or threatening the person or property. These powers come from the decisions of judges over the centuries known as the 'common law' and not from any Act of Parliament.

Whilst the powers to deal with a breach of the peace are important (and in practical terms the power to enter premises is a very valuable one), they are seldom used these days; the problem being that you can only detain a person as long as is necessary to prevent the breach of the peace. In practice the person has almost certainly committed a substantial offence for which they can be arrested, provided the necessity test has been met and, most certainly, can be brought before a court. These criminal offences range from simply being drunk in a public place through to harassment, causing an affray, and finally rioting; to say nothing of any actual assault that may have taken place.

Whilst the police may have extensive powers to deal with individual cases of public disorder, it has now been recognised that the job of keeping the peace, preventing crime and disorder and ensuring quality of life in the community cannot be left to the police alone. The task is both too big and too complex. That is why we now have initiatives like the Community Crime and Disorder Reduction Partnerships, as discussed in Chapter 6.

What follows in the next two chapters is an introduction to some key principles of the criminal law and a brief examination of some of the more common offences you will be expected to deal with on a day-to-day basis. It will give you a taste for the type of knowledge you will need to gain and it will help to build the foundations for any further training you undertake.

FURTHER READING

→ <http://www.criminal-courts-review.org.uk>
On this site you will find the review of the criminal courts carried out in 2001. It's a fascinating read, not least because it gives a view of the workings of the courts from 'the other side'. It is also kept reasonably up to date with information about the ongoing reform of the court system.

→ Rebecca Huxley-Binns, *Unlocking the English Legal System*, 2005, Hodder Arnold

17

A QUICK LESSON IN CRIME

We have hinted at this elsewhere but it is worth stating again here formally because it is so important. There are two main reasons why, as a police officer, you need to know the detail of all common criminal offences:

- because you need to know what you will need to prove;
- because you need to recognise if an offence has been committed, and if so what type, so you know what powers are available to you.

A police officer who doesn't know the intricacies of at least the everyday offences is like a carpenter who does not know how to use a plane—ineffective.

Even though every criminal offence is, like a recipe, made up of its own particular ingredients (such as theft, whose ingredients include dishonesty, the taking of someone else's property and the intention to permanently deprive the owner of it), there are some basic principles that apply in nearly all circumstances. Let's look at those first.

17.1 Guilty knowledge

There is a rule in the criminal law that actions alone cannot amount to a crime; they have to be accompanied by an intention to do wrong—or at least a realisation that their actions are wrong. This intention is known as the 'guilty mind' or 'guilty knowledge'. The Latin term that is sometimes still used is '*mens rea*'.

There are some offences where a guilty mind is not required, generally road traffic offences, such as speeding. These are known as absolute offences. However, as a general rule you can assume that only if someone had the intention to do wrong when they carried out their actions can they be liable for 'committing a crime'. An example of this principle in action would be if, while you were out shopping today, your mind was on other things (like a new career in the police), and you wandered out of the shop without paying for the goods you were holding, you would not have stolen them. Your actions in leaving the shop without paying would not be enough to make you guilty of theft, because you had no wrongful intention—no guilty mind. This rule protects people who may have some mental impairment or who are not capable of understanding the consequences of their actions. It also protects people whose innocent actions go wrong—or just those who go through life in a daydream (you can now probably understand why speeding is an absolute offence—if it wasn't nobody could ever be convicted).

ATTENTION TO DETAIL

One common situation where people may not know what they are doing is when they are drunk. So does this mean that drunkenness amounts to 'blameless behaviour'? The answer is, 'No'—if not knowing what you were doing because you were drunk gave you a general 'get out of jail free' card, how many people would ever be convicted of anything, especially crimes involving public order and violence?

There are special rules for drunkenness—generally you cannot avoid conviction for most crimes simply by showing you were too drunk or too 'high' on drugs to know what you were doing, but, as always, there are some exceptions.

For some offences it is not necessary to show that the person intended to do wrong, merely that they were reckless as to whether their actions would do harm. There are many different mental states that meet the requirements of different offences. However, as a general rule some degree of 'guilty mind' is needed.

17.2 **Wrongful acts**

The other key element that is needed is the 'wrongful act'. This may sound obvious but it isn't always. Simply having a guilty mind or intention to do wrong can never, on its own, amount to a crime. If bad thoughts were a crime we would all be in a lot of trouble. To prove that a person committed a crime you have to prove that they did the relevant wrongful act as well. Using our example of the theft again, we would need to show that they actually took the property.

The other thing you need to note about the 'wrongful act' is that you have to show that the person did the act voluntarily, that they were in control of their movements at the time. For example, if you had a sneezing fit whilst driving your car and, as a result, crashed into another car, you could not be held responsible for driving badly.

There are a few offences where, rather than having to prove the person did something they should not have, you will need to prove they did not do something that they should have done. There aren't many of these offences because generally the law is about stopping people doing bad things not forcing them to do good. However, there are a few occasions where a person will commit a crime by failing to act. These are usually where a person has a legal duty or a special relationship towards another person. Examples here would be parents neglecting their children, or a police officer who fails to at least try to prevent an assault.

17.3 **Unfinished offences**

Staying with the idea of criminal acts, we need to look at a special group of crimes—'incomplete' or unfinished offences. These are offences where, for one reason or another, the person committing them doesn't manage to achieve what they have set out to do. Let us look at an example.

> ### EXAMPLE
>
> A woman puts her handbag down on a seat in a night club. Someone decides to try to steal a purse from inside the bag. He puts his hand into the bag only to find that there is no purse in it. The woman sees him and tells the club manager, who then calls the police and asks if an offence has been committed. If you took the call what would you say?

Well as a starting point, look at the issue of 'guilty mind'. The man clearly intended to steal so we are over the first hurdle. Now look at the wrongful act. Did he, whilst in full control of his body, carry out a wrongful act? Most certainly he did, he put his hand in the bag. The fact that he was unable to complete the offence was due to the fact that there was no purse to steal, something he did not know at the time he formed his guilty mind and carried out the wrongful act. In these circumstances the offence is said to have been 'attempted', and the law treats the person guilty of attempted crimes in exactly the same way as if the offence had been completed, and they are liable to exactly the same punishment. So the answer to the club manager's question would be that an offence had indeed been committed: the offence of 'attempted theft'.

17.4 **Defences**

When considering criminal offences, it is important to think of what *defences* the accused person might have. Some serious crimes have specific defences written into them, while all have some possible form of defence. As a police officer you need to know about the defences just as much as the points to prove. Why? Well there are two main reasons:

- because the police have a duty to investigate crimes fairly and impartially—if there is evidence that supports a person's defence then you need to collect it just as diligently as evidence that points to his or her guilt;

- because if you don't know what the defences are you will not be able to deal with them when you come to interview the accused person.

17.5 **Proof**

'Proof' is a little word with big consequences. Remember that a person can only be convicted of a criminal offence if there is proof of each and every ingredient of that offence. Criminal trials in England and Wales are not about what actually happened—they are about whether the prosecution can prove the guilt of the accused.

There are only three ways of proving a person's involvement in a criminal offence:

- witnesses
- admission by the individual
- forensic evidence.

And the greatest of the three is forensic evidence. Witnesses can be forgetful, mistaken, dishonest or just unreliable, especially when it comes to identification evidence, and they can go to pieces under cross-examination. Additionally jurors sometimes disbelieve them for no other reason than their appearance. Admissions are more reliable than they used to be now that solicitors sit in on almost every interview, but they cannot always be obtained and they can always be withdrawn. Forensic evidence, however, is hard and tangible, the jury can see it and it's very difficult for the defence to attack solid physical evidence—provided it has been properly and lawfully collected and presented. The ideal, of course, is to have all three types of evidence, all saying the same thing, but that seldom happens.

As pointed out above it is not the job of the police simply to collect evidence against the accused person. They must collect all the evidence relating to the crime, impartially and efficiently, and present it to the Crown Prosecution Service (CPS). It is the CPS that will make the decision whether or not to take the person before the courts and will manage the entire process.

In gathering and presenting evidence there are two key rules to remember.

The first rule

The defendant does not have to prove that they did not commit the offence; it is the prosecution's job to prove that they did. Everyone is innocent unless and until they are proved guilty. A famous judge once described this as being the 'golden thread' that ran throughout the criminal justice system. You may also recall that this rule is enshrined in Article 6 of the European Convention on Human Rights (see Chapter 13).

The second rule

The prosecution must present enough evidence and sufficiently strong evidence to prove the defendant's guilt beyond reasonable doubt. It is not enough to be able to show that it is likely that the defendant committed the offence or even that it is probable that they did so. The court will not convict unless they are *sure*—beyond reasonable doubt—that the defendant is guilty.

17.6 **Remember the victim**

For every crime there is at least one victim. Crime does not just happen; it involves real people suffering real loss and real harm. Even in what are wrongly called 'victimless' crimes (such as the possession of drugs and offences relating to prostitution) people are still being hurt—often the offenders themselves, and certainly the well-being of the community at large is damaged.

Certain victims are especially vulnerable, such as those that are too old, too young or otherwise unable to look after themselves. People who have been the victim of crimes on more than one occasion, known in police parlance as 'repeat victims', also fall into the category of vulnerable victims.

Crime can be a fascinating subject and studying it will throw up all sorts of scenarios and variations. Investigating it is even more engrossing. Whether studying or investigating, it is very easy to become detached and clinical. So you need always to remember the victim and be sympathetic to their needs.

Now that you know what a crime is and the basics of proof, in the next chapter we will look at the common offences that, as a police officer, you will have to deal with.

FURTHER READING

→ Christopher Allen, *Practical Guide to Evidence*, 2004, Cavendish Publishing Ltd

18

LAW AND ORDER: A CLOSER LOOK

Having now briefly examined the principles that underpin the criminal law, it is time to look at some specific offences in more detail. The ones we will look at are those which as a street-duty officer you can expect to have to deal with on a regular basis and some of them almost every day.

18.1 Offences against property

The majority of all crimes committed in England and Wales involve property in some way. Although there is evidence to suggest that the incidence of some of these offences is falling they are still very prevalent; as a police officer they will make up the majority of your caseload. Indeed, the offence of 'theft' accounts for around half of all recorded crime on its own.

Property crime not only covers the stealing of other people's property; it also includes damaging and destroying property, breaking into homes, business premises and schools, and taking vehicles without the owner's consent before subsequently abandoning them. If you think back to Chapter 13, you may recall that the peaceful enjoyment of one's possessions is a fundamental human right that is protected by the European Convention (Protocol 1 Article 1).

Property crime is the cause of a great deal of misery and distress to the victims. Not only does it bring unhappiness and expense to the people whose property has been stolen or damaged, property crime also:

- has an enormous impact on the economy (every price in every major shop is a little higher than it otherwise would be and every credit card charges a little extra interest to cover the costs of fraud);

- creates fear of crime in many communities and so damages the quality of life for everyone;

- uses up a considerable amount of police time and resources.

Some property crimes—such as burglary—can include injury or harm to the occupier of the property as well. As a result of all of the above, most property crimes carry substantial prison sentences. So let's look at some of the main property crimes.

Theft

A good starting place when looking at property crime is theft. Not only, as we have seen, is it the most common offence, but it is pretty straightforward and introduces within its ingredients concepts that we will find related elsewhere.

You may think that you have a fair idea of what is involved in an offence of theft. So why not take a couple of minutes, before reading on, to note down what you think the ingredients are?

In police training, offences are given as 'definitions' which include the 'points to prove' (the ingredients). They are not normally just a copy of the section from the Act of Parliament; instead they use phrases in standard English so that they become more meaningful and easier to remember. Learning definitions by heart is a useful way making sure you have the core knowledge you need on the streets immediately available to you. For that reason many forces insist that all new recruits learn the definitions of key offences and also those that relate to the most used police powers. So, whilst we won't do this for every offence we will look at, let's give you some practice; this is the definition of theft:

A person is guilty of theft if they:

Dishonestly appropriate property belonging to another with the intention of permanently depriving the other of it.

Thief and steal shall be construed accordingly.

Section 1 of the Theft Act 1968, maximum penalty on indictment 7 years, triable either way.

There in a nutshell you have the offence of theft. Of course learning definitions by heart is not much use unless you know what they mean, so let's look at the points to prove.

Dishonestly

In this context, and in most definitions where you see it, 'dishonestly' means that the person behaved in a way that would be seen by the average citizen as dishonest. Section 2 of the Act sets out three sets of circumstances in which the person's action would not be regarded as dishonest—remember we spoke in the previous chapter about defences. You will learn about these in your initial training, so there is no need to go into them here.

Appropriates

Most thefts involve someone simply taking something. However, there are circumstances where a person dishonestly gets ownership of someone else's property without actually 'taking' it. Consequently in section 3 of the Act, 'appropriates' is defined to mean assuming the rights of ownership.

Property

It seems obvious that you can only commit theft if you actually take something. The problem comes when we look at what that 'something' could be. How about the balance in your bank account? That doesn't actually exist as a physical thing—it's only a record in a computer database, but you would be rather upset if someone took it away from you. How would you feel if, whilst out walking, you picked some mushrooms that were growing wild in a field intending to cook them for your dinner and you were promptly arrested for theft? You can see how complex the idea of property is when it comes to theft. Consequently, we will just note that a bank balance can be stolen but mushrooms growing wild cannot (unless you do it for gain or reward) and, for now, leave it at that.

Belonging to another

Again it probably seems obvious that you cannot steal your own property. Well, actually in law there are certain circumstances where you can, but you can ignore these for now. Generally speaking you need to prove that the property belonged to someone other than the person appropriating it and that they knew this to be the case (remember the guilty mind?).

Intention to permanently deprive

This is essential and sometimes it can be the hardest part to prove. If someone takes something belonging to someone else but intends to give it back, whole and complete, and at a later date, then they will not have committed theft. For this reason there is a specific offence which deals with taking a vehicle without permission and later abandoning it, which we will look at in a moment.

At this point, how did your 'layperson's' view of what theft was about compare to the real thing? Probably, if you were like most people, you had the sense of it but not the detail.

If evidence to prove any one of the above points is missing then you have not got an offence of theft (or at least not one you can prove). However, there may well be one of many other crimes that would fit your circumstances and which, perhaps, are provable. At this point an example may help.

EXAMPLE

Petra, a college student, runs out of milk and doesn't have the money, at the moment, to buy any more. She sees some bottles of milk on the doorstep of the house opposite. So she takes a bottle of milk intending to use it with her breakfast but also to replace it with some other milk later that day. Someone sees her and calls the police. If you were the police officer what would you do?

You know what the points to prove are for an offence of theft, so let's look at each in turn. The first problem is to decide whether Petra was dishonest. If she knows the neighbours well enough, it might have been that she thought they would have given her permission to take the milk had she asked them, and in law this might well provide her with a defence. On the other hand perhaps she knows them well enough to know they would have refused, which might be why she did not ask. So we can note that this is an area that we will have to explore in interview. We certainly can't prove this point yet, but we do have enough to afford sufficient suspicion that we can carry on. The next point is, has she 'appropriated' the milk? Yes she has; she walked across the road and took it. That fact that it belonged to another is also straightforward. The final point is the intention to permanently deprive, can we prove this? Well, yes we can, depending on what she has done with the milk by the time we arrive. We may need to clarify the point in interview but her intention was to use the milk with her breakfast. That would mean that she had permanently deprived the owner of it. The fact that she intended to replace the milk with another bottle is irrelevant; even if she did so it would not have been the same milk. So we have sufficient evidence to afford reasonable grounds to suspect Petra is guilty of theft and, depending what she says in interview on the subject of dishonesty, the case is capable of being proved.

Robbery

Now that you understand theft, you are most of the way to understanding robbery. People sometimes use the term 'robbing' in relation to shops, cars, and buildings. They may say something like, 'I have had my car robbed' or 'They robbed her house last week'. In fact, and in law, only people can be robbed. Robbery is simply a theft which is accompanied by violence or the threat of violence to a person. If there is no theft there is no robbery—though there may be an attempt (remember 'unfinished offences' from the last chapter) or an offence of assault. Robbery can range from an incident in which a mobile phone is snatched and force or threats of force are used towards the owner, to an armed hold-up of a bank or security van.

The key additional ingredient is that the use of force, or the threat to use immediate force, must precede the theft and be used or threatened in order that the theft can take place. It is not necessary that the force be used or offered to the owner of the property but it must be against a person who is actually present. There is no need for a weapon to be used, nor is there an offence of armed robbery or robbery with violence (though the presence of any of these three things will affect the sentence handed down by the court). Robbery is a very serious offence and can only be tried in the Crown Court.

Burglary

Just as only people can be robbed, only *buildings* can be burgled. Burglary is a more complicated offence than theft or robbery. However, there are some key features that, once you understand them, will make everything clear.

First there are two types of burglary: one deals with the offender's intentions at the time they enter the building, whilst the other deals with the burglar's actions once inside the building. Grasp this and it is pretty well straightforward.

Type 1: Intentions

The ingredients of the first type of burglary are:

- entering a building (or a part of a building) — this can include reaching through an open window or leaning through a door;

- as a trespasser — we looked at what this meant back in Chapter 15 so we don't need to repeat it here. Note that it is possible to enter premises with full permission but either go into a part of the building where you don't have permission, or remain concealed until after your permission has expired — in both cases one can become a trespasser even though the original entry was lawful;

- intending to do one or more of three other crimes, i.e. —
  - steal
  - inflict serious injury on anyone inside
  - cause damage to the property or anything in it.

Note that this is a crime of *intention*, the burglar does not have to carry out any theft etc. — it is enough that he or she intended to do so at the time they entered the building, or part of a building, as a trespasser. You might want to think about how you could prove to a court that a person had the required intention, look back at the section on proof in the last chapter and refresh your memory of the three types of evidence and think about how you could, perhaps, use each to prove the point. Of course if the burglar actually goes on to carry out one of the three offences that would be pretty good supporting evidence of their intention at the time of entry. If they do go on to steal or inflict serious injury on someone inside the building, then they commit the second type of burglary.

Type 2: Behaviour after entering

The second type of burglary is concerned with what the offender does after entering the building or part of a building as a trespasser. If they steal anything (or try to) or inflict serious injury on anyone inside the building (or try to), they commit this offence. There is no requirement to have to prove any intention on behalf of the offender.

You can see that there is a big overlap between the two types of burglary and often both will have been committed in the same set of circumstances. Another example may be needed.

EXAMPLE

A man who has gone into a pub for a drink with friends visits the toilets. He hides in the toilets until the pub has closed, when he goes back into the bar room and takes a bottle of whiskey and some cigarettes from behind the bar. The landlord hears a noise from the bar and calls the police. What offence do you think might have been committed and why?

The starting point in deciding whether the man has committed either type of burglary is whether or not he was a trespasser. At the time the man went into the toilets he was a customer of the pub and had permission to be there—like all the people using the pub—so he wasn't then trespassing. However, once the pub closed, the man no longer had the permission and he now became a trespasser. Once he re-enters the bar area the first part of the offence is complete; he has entered a part of a building as a trespasser. The question to be answered now is what his intention was at that time. If he intended to steal the cigarettes and whiskey then he was guilty of the first type of burglary. When he takes the goods from behind the bar he dishonestly appropriates property belonging to the landlord, intending to permanently deprive him of it. We know this is theft and so the man is guilty, at this point in time, of the second type of burglary.

ATTENTION TO DETAIL

Did you realise that, even if the pub had still been open when he took the property, he did not have permission to go behind the bar and therefore was a trespasser at this point anyway?

Burglary is a serious offence that can have considerable impact on the victims—especially if the building involved is their home. It's worth remembering what was said earlier about the victims of crime. The effect of burglary on people's feeling of security, and that of their families, can be devastating. The burglary of homes (known in police parlance as 'burglary dwelling') is treated by the courts as a particularly serious crime.

Taking vehicles

We saw earlier that if the offender dishonestly takes someone else's property but has no intention of permanently depriving the owner of it the offence of theft has not been committed. So if someone without your permission takes your mobile phone, perhaps for a prank, and then, without using it, leaves it in the next office, they have not committed any offence. However, if someone takes your car without your permission and leaves it in the next street then they have committed an offence under section 12 of the Theft Act 1968, taking a motor vehicle or other conveyance without authority.

This offence is known by many names in different parts of the country and across different police forces: 'unlawful taking of a motor vehicle

(UTMV)', 'taking and driving away (TDA)' and 'taking without consent (TWOC)' are probably the most common variations. Another name commonly used in some newspapers is 'joy riding'. There is nothing joyous about this offence. It creates fear, frustration and expense to the owner and the community—not to mention the large numbers of people every year who are killed and injured by criminals driving cars that they have taken without the consent of the owner. There is a further, aggravated, form of this offence that occurs when the vehicle is used in certain incidents before the owner gets it back. This carries a longer sentence than the six months that the 'basic' offence can attract.

The offence of taking vehicles does have a statutory defence. If the person who took the vehicle believed that:

• they had a lawful authority to use the vehicle, or
• the owner would have consented had they known of the taking *and* the circumstances of it.

To see what this second defence could mean in practice let's look at another example.

EXAMPLE

A student living in a hall of residence usually allows a fellow resident to use her motor bike to go to the gym every Tuesday and Thursday. One Tuesday our student could not be found by her fellow resident and so he took the bike anyway. After all, he thought, he only wanted to go to the gym as usual and the owner had always let him use the bike for that. The owner comes back and finds that the bike is missing. She calls the police for advice and you take the call. What would you tell her?

First, has the fellow student taken the motor bike? The answer is 'Yes'. Next, did he have the owners consent? Well, not specifically; however, he believed that if he had asked her if he could borrow the bike to go to the gym she would have said yes because he had regularly been given permission to do so in the past. For this reason he has a full defence and does not commit the offence. If he had taken the bike to go on an amateur motor-cross rally, then it would have been a different matter entirely.

As a final note, it is also an offence to get a lift with someone when you know they have taken the conveyance without the owner's consent.

Going equipped

Imagine that you are a police officer on patrol late one evening in an area where there have been a lot of burglaries, when a member of the public points out a man to you and says he saw him behaving suspiciously near the side door of a locked shop. He further says that when the man saw him he seemed to put something inside his coat and walk away quite quickly. You quite rightly stop and search the man and find in an inside pocket a tyre lever and some thin rubber gloves. What can you do about it? Well these are precisely the sort of circumstances that the offence of 'going equipped' was designed to deal with.

Under section 25 of the Theft Act 1968 it is an offence for any person, when not at their home address, to have in their possession any article for use in connection with or in the course of any burglary, theft or cheat (by which it is meant a deception offence under section 15 of the Act). 'Articles' here mean anything that the person intended to use in the commission of one of the three types of offence. Examples would be screwdrivers, knives, gloves, disguises or false credit cards. So in our example the evidence provided by the member of the public together with the spate of burglaries in the area would be sufficient to prove that the man had possession at that time of the tyre lever and gloves intending to use them in connection with a burglary.

Proving intention, as we have seen, can be tricky. So you will be pleased to hear that if the article was made or adapted for use in the commission of one of the three offences, then that is sufficient proof—there is no need to worry about the intention of the suspect.

So the mere possession of a forged credit card outside of one's home address would constitute an offence.

'Going equipped' is a very useful tool for the street-duty officer and what is even better is it enables you to deal with criminals *before* they have committed a crime which harms a victim.

Criminal damage

As we have already seen, the European Convention on Human Rights affords people the right to the peaceful enjoyment of their possessions. The protection of the right can be seen in the property offences above. However, it also extends to protecting possessions from damage and destruction. There are several criminal offences that relate to this.

The main law containing the relevant offences is the Criminal Damage Act 1971. Section 1 makes it an offence to deliberately or recklessly damage someone else's property unless you have a lawful excuse. An example of a lawful excuse would be a police officer who damages a door whilst making correct use of one of their powers to enter a building.

That it is an offence to damage someone else's property is probably to be expected. However, it is also an offence to damage your own property in circumstances where, deliberately or recklessly, someone else's life would be endangered. Perhaps an example would be someone who chopped down a large tree in their garden in such a manner that caused it to fall into a busy road. Even if nobody was hurt, such an act would constitute an offence under the Criminal Damage Act. Criminal damage offences where fire is used are known as arson.

The Act also makes it an offence to threaten to damage or destroy property and to have in your possession articles to be used for damaging or destroying property. So a threat to smash up someone's home or car is an offence in itself, as is having a tin of aerosol paint with which to spray graffiti. Again these are useful offences for the street-duty officer and ones which seem to be somewhat under-used by many.

'Aggravated damage' happens when the offender damages property and intends to endanger someone's life or is reckless as to whether life would be endangered. An example of this very serious offence would be throwing a brick through the windscreen of a moving car. Aggravated damage offences often involve the use of fire (examples of people putting petrol through someone's letter box followed by a lighted match appear all too often in the press) and this is the most serious form of criminal damage—it carries a maximum penalty of life imprisonment.

Racially or religiously aggravated offences

For many years there has been particular concern at the additional evil of crimes that were specifically aimed at racial groups or which were motivated by hostility towards a person's racial origin. The Crime and Disorder Act 1998 revisited the issue of racially aggravated crime. The result was the identification of a number of offences that would be treated as being far more serious by the police and the courts if they are shown to be racially aggravated. This was subsequently extended to include religiously aggravated offences.

Generally an offence will be deemed to be racially or religiously aggravated if:

- at the time of committing it (or immediately before/after), the offender demonstrated towards the victim hostility based on the victim's membership of a racial or religious group, or

- the offence was motivated by hostility towards members of a racial or religious group based on their membership of that group.

Criminal damage is an offence that can be racially or religiously aggravated. The other offences include assaults and some offences relating to public disorder.

18.2 **Offences against people**

The next group of offences to consider are those committed directly against people. Generally these are categorised according to the amount of injury that the assailant caused or intended to cause to their victim. At the lowest end of the scale we have common assault, where no lasting injury is done, and at the top we have manslaughter and murder—though these last two are outside the scope of this book.

Generally speaking, offences against people involve assaults (and also what is technically known as battery—the actual application of physical force). If unlawful force (or a real threat of it) is used towards another person an offence will have been committed. The next step is to decide which one and, as we have said, this is determined by the amount of injury caused.

If no lasting injury is caused—nothing much more than, perhaps, a temporary reddening of the skin—then it will be a common assault. You should note that the normal accidental knocking against or unintended jostling against other people will not amount to an assault. There has to be a deliberate use of force. If the injury is a little more serious, say a black eye or a minor cut, then it would be an offence of 'assault occasioning actual bodily harm' under section 47 of the Offences Against the Person Act 1861. If the injury involves a serious cut or a broken bone or other serious harm, you would be looking at an offence of 'causing grievous bodily harm or wounding' under section 20 of the 1861 Act, unless the assailant intended to cause such a level of injury, in which case it would be an offence under section 18 and regarded by the courts as much more serious (it carries a maximum penalty of life imprisonment). All three levels of assault can be racially or religiously motivated.

18.3 **Offences against the peace**

In this section we will take a look at those offences relating to the disturbance of people's peaceful enjoyment of their private, public or community life. As a street-duty officer, particularly if you are working in a town centre, you will get to know these offences very well and very quickly.

Our starting point is the breach of the peace. This is not an offence as such, though as we saw in Chapter 15 you can be detained if you are committing one and it does provide a very handy power of entry for the astute officer. However, as was mentioned, if a person is committing a breach of the peace, particularly in a public place, they are probably committing a substantial offence and it is almost always better to use that to deal with the person and the situation. So let's look at the substantial offences that may be open to us.

The Act that we are concerned with here is the Public Order Act 1986. As with assaults this act provides a number of offences of increasing severity. At the bottom of the chain we have the offence under section 5, 'occasioning harassment alarm and distress'.

Section 5—Harassment, alarm and distress

This offence is committed when a person:

- uses threatening, abusive or insulting words or behaviour, or disorderly behaviour, or

- displays any writing, sign or other visible representation which is threatening, abusive or insulting,

within the hearing or sight of a person likely to be caused harassment, alarm or distress thereby. This offence is used in cases which amount to less serious incidents of anti-social behaviour. Where violence has been used, unless it was of a very minor nature, it is not normally appropriate. There must be a person within the sight or hearing of

199

the offender who is likely to be caused harassment, alarm or distress by the conduct in question. Although in strict theory this could be a police officer, in practice you will not get a conviction if the only people that were likely to be harassed etc. were the police. Additionally you need to be aware that although you need to prove that there was such a person who was likely to have been caused harassment, alarm or distress, there is no requirement for them to actually provide evidence to that effect. Your own observations of the reactions of members of the public to the incident will usually be enough. This offence can be racially and religiously aggravated.

Section 4a — Intentional harassment, alarm or distress

This offence was added in as an afterthought by the Criminal Justice and Public Order Act 1994. It is the next one up the scale from section 5 and its provisions are identical except that under this offence you have to prove that the language or behaviour was used or the sign was displayed with the *intention* of causing harassment, alarm or distress. This offence can be racially and religiously aggravated.

Section 4 — Fear or provocation of violence

This offence is regarded as equal in severity to section 4a and this time the person using the insulting words and behaviour etc. must do so with *intent* to cause a person to believe that immediate unlawful violence will be used or with the intent to provoke another into the immediate use of unlawful violence. This offence can be racially and religiously aggravated.

Section 3 — Affray

The offence of affray occurs where a person uses or threatens unlawful violence towards another and this conduct would cause a person of reasonable firmness present at the scene to fear for his or her personal safety. The seriousness of this offence lies in the effect the conduct of the offender has on persons other than the person towards whom he is directing his violence. Some third party, uninvolved in the violence, must be put in fear for this offence to be complete. The Crown Prosecution Service advise that suitable circumstances for charging an offence of affray would include:

> A fight between two or more people in a place where members of the general public are present (for example in a public house, discotheque, restaurant or street) with a level of violence such as would put them in substantial fear (as opposed to passing concern) for their safety (even though the fighting is not directed towards them).

Section 2 — Violent disorder

Violent disorder is very similar to affray except that there must be at least three people who are acting together in a concerted act of violence. This offence is really designed to deal with fights between rival gangs, and, as such, a street-duty officer is not likely to come across it very often. That said, when there is serious public disorder at a public event (such as a football match) and violence is used towards the police this may well be a suitable charge for those arrested.

Section 1 — Riot

Conduct which falls under the offence of riot is thankfully very rare. It requires that at least 12 people be acting together and using violence for a common purpose and that the conduct of them taken together was such that it did cause a person of reasonable firmness present at the scene to fear for his or her personal safety. The Crown Prosecution Service will normally only proceed with a charge of riot in the most serious cases usually linked to planned or spontaneous serious outbreaks of sustained violence.

Offensive and anti-social behaviour

Aside from the substantive offences we have looked at, another measure to deal with offensive and anti-social behaviour that is open to the police is the 'anti-social behaviour order' more commonly known by its initials 'ASBO'. ASBOs are an order made by a civil court that requires the named person to refrain from specific behaviour or associating with named individuals or going to a specified area. They last for a minimum period of two years, and can be served on anyone over ten years old. The intention of the order is to protect the public from further harm rather than to punish the offender, so the issuing of an ASBO does not count as a criminal conviction. Neither is it necessary that the person has been convicted of any offence—though in practice the court will require evidence of persistent anti-social behaviour before making an order and what better evidence than a string of relevant convictions. If the person breaches their order they then commit a criminal offence for which they can be arrested and punished.

There are also several offences that have been listed as being particularly common—and particularly disruptive to the public peace. As such these offences have been singled out as being suitable to be dealt with by issuing fixed penalty notices, both by constables and other designated people (e.g. police community support officers). In summary these offences are:

- section 5 of the Public Order Act (see above);
- throwing stones at trains;
- dropping litter;
- making nuisance phone calls;
- wasting police time.

The use of fixed penalty notices, once reserved for minor traffic offences such as parking, has gained a lot of support in Government circles in recent years and you can expect the list of offences for which they can be used to be extended further.

Drunkenness

Any experienced street-duty officer will tell you that most of the violence and anti-social behaviour that occurs on the streets is fuelled by alcohol, and this has been borne out by official studies. Therefore it should be no surprise that the police have powers relating to drink.

There is a particular offence of being drunk and disorderly and all that needs to be proved is that the person was behaving in a disorderly way whilst drunk in a public place. Interestingly, when it comes to proof that a person was in fact drunk, the word of a constable is deemed sufficient—the courts have always held that in the matters of drink and drunkenness police officers are experts!

The police also have a power under the Confiscation of Alcohol (Young Persons) Act 1997. In brief this says that, where a constable reasonably suspects that a person in a public place is in possession of alcohol and that:

- the person is under the age of 18, or
- the person intends that the drink should be drunk by a person under the age of 18, or
- a person under the age of 18 who is with that person has recently consumed alcohol,

the constable may require the person to surrender anything that is in their possession that the constable reasonably believes to be alcohol and to state their name and address.

There are further offences and powers that allow the police to deal with drunkenness and street drinking in areas that have been specially designated by the local authority. You may have seen notices specifying such places. More senior police officers have additional powers to order premises to be closed where there is anti-social behaviour involving the sale of alcohol.

18.4 **Offences against policy**

Some criminal offences aren't committed against any particular person or property though, as we have already discussed, such crimes still have victims. For the purposes of this book we will categorise these crimes as 'offences against policy', because the fact that the behaviour is illegal has been decided by the policies of the Government of the day. These offences cover various areas of human behaviour from certain sexual acts where all the parties are consenting, to the possession of weapons and drugs. The last two are good examples of what we mean by offences against policy, because it was not that long ago when the possession of a weapon, even a firearm, in a public place was not an offence and the possession and use of all drugs was perfectly legal—you could buy heroin at Boots the Chemist.

Controlled drugs

The use of controlled drugs is the root cause of a great deal of crime. A recent study revealed that no fewer than 80 per cent of the prisoners in a local county prison were drug users or had been sentenced for a drug-related crime, and fully 40 per cent of all women in prison have been sentenced for drug offences (possession, importation or trafficking). It is also notable that a large proportion of thefts (particularly shoplifting) and burglaries are committed by people who are trying to obtain money to buy drugs. Furthermore, the criminal gangs seeking to protect the area in which they have a monopoly on the drug trade from other gangs frequently resort to extreme violence, including murder. Such violence too often involves the innocent. Even as far back as the mid-1990s about 90 per cent of the work of the National Criminal Intelligence Service was related to the drug trade.

Not that long ago drugs were a problem only in some areas of larger cities; they are now available in every town and large village in the country, and the crime and social problems have spread accordingly. The total cost to the country of the drug trade is tens, possibly over a hundred, of billions of pounds every year. As a police officer this is an area of the law you will quickly be involved in.

Controlled drugs are divided into three categories or classes: A, B and C. The decision about which class a substance should belong to depends on its effect on the individual using it. Class A drugs are the most dangerous and include heroin, cocaine, LSD and ecstasy; in Class B are barbiturates and other amphetamines; Class C drugs, the least harmful, now includes cannabis which has been downgraded from Class B. The category of a particular drug determines the maximum sentence that can be handed down by the courts and so, before powers of arrest were standardised by the Serious Organised Crime and Police Act (which we met in Chapter 14), was of particular interest to every officer. Now you need not be terribly concerned.

There are three main drug offences that you will be involved in:

- simple possession—where the drug is intended for personal use or no other purpose can be proved;
- possession with intent to supply the drug to someone else;
- supplying or offering to supply someone else with a controlled drug.

There are other offences involving the production and importation of controlled drugs, but as a street-duty police officer you are not likely to have to deal with these and so they are outside the scope of this book.

In practical terms if you find someone in possession of a quantity of, say, white powder you will not know if it is heroin or washing powder. Therefore most arrests for drug offences are made on the basis of reasonable suspicion and charges are only made after the substance has been analysed.

Weapons

The carrying of weapons has become an issue of considerable concern over recent years. In particular, the use of knives in crime has caused some notable changes in the law. For these reasons, the powers to stop and search people that we discussed in Chapter 15 were made available to the police in relation to weapons.

Generally the law makes a distinction between knives and similar articles and other sorts of weapons. Firearms are a particular group of weapons that attract very strict controls and these are outside the scope this book, though, as a rule, it will be an offence for most people to have handguns, rifles, shotguns or ammunition for any of them unless they have specific authority to do so.

Although you may be familiar with terms such as 'offensive weapon', the law in this area is wide and complex, going far beyond making it an offence to have such items. Some legislation is aimed at preventing people carrying certain weapons, while in other areas it is concerned with the sale or use of weapons. For now all you need to know is that it is an offence for a person to have an offensive weapon with them in a public place without lawful authority or reasonable excuse.

What is an offensive weapon? Well, it is defined as being something that has been made or adapted or is intended for causing injury to someone else. An example of something made for causing injury would be a bayonet. As with the offence of going equipped, unless the article has been made or adapted for causing injury you are going to have to prove intention.

EXAMPLE

Police officers carrying batons whilst on duty, or members of the armed forces carrying bayonets on parade, have offensive weapons with them

continued

---

continued

in a public place. However, they have 'lawful authority'. Similarly, people having the tools of their trade with them in the course of their work (e.g. Stanley knives for fitting carpets) would probably have a 'reasonable excuse'—as long as they didn't carry them intending to use them for causing injury.

There is also an offence of carrying a knife or other bladed or sharply pointed instrument in a public place (or on school premises) without good reason or lawful authority. For this offence there is no requirement that the person had the item with them for a particular purpose, mere possession in public is enough. There is, though, an exception for small pen-knives provided the cutting edge of the blade is not longer than 3 inches (7.72 cm).

ATTENTION TO DETAIL

If a person is found to have a sharpened stick with them in the street there are two offences that need to be considered. The sharpened stick could be regarded as an 'offensive weapon' (something adapted for causing injury). On the other hand it is most certainly a pointed article. In both cases you would need to ascertain whether the person had lawful authority or a good reason for having the stick in their possession at that time.

As mentioned previously, there are other offences aimed at restricting the supply of weapons and their availability in England and Wales. In particular there is a specific offence relating to the sale of knives to people under the age of 16.

In this chapter you have learned some of the basics about the most common offences a street-duty officer has to deal with. This will have given you a flavour for the extent of knowledge the ordinary constable has to have to do their job properly and if you do join the Service, you will have a flying start in the theoretical aspect of your initial training.

FURTHER READING

→ <http://www.blackstonespolicemanuals.com>
Blackstone's are the main publishers of the standard police textbooks.

→ <http://www.opsi.gov.uk>

The Economic and Social Costs of Class A Drug Use in England and Wales, Home Office research study No 249, 2000

Appendix 1

GLOSSARY OF POLICE TERMS

Like many jobs the police service has its own informal language; you will learn a whole new vocabulary when you join. Within this vocabulary, many shorthand expressions have developed in the police setting. Nicknames, letters and abbreviations—even numbers—the police language can be very confusing when it is first encountered. Although the list below contains some of the more common references used in the police, some expressions differ from one force to another.

Organisations and agencies

ACPO Association of Chief Police Officers. All chief officers from Home Office police forces and the chief officers of the Police Service for Northern Ireland belong to ACPO. It provides many different advisory committees (e.g. on firearms, training and crime) and contributes to debates on important issues such as drugs, policies and sex offenders.

ACPOS Same as ACPO but for Scotland.

ACPOD Nothing like ACPO. Association of Chief Police Officers' Drivers.

APA Association of Police Authorities.

BPA Black Police Association. Provides support and advice for all police officers and managers in relation to issues of ethnicity and race. There is a national BPA, as well as a growing number of force BPAs.

GPA Gay Police Association. Provides support and advice for all police officers and managers in relation to relevant issues.

HMIC Her Majesty's Inspectorate of Constabulary. A body of senior people (some of them retired Chief Constables) appointed by the Crown who inspect police forces and publish reports on what they find. There is a Chief

Inspector of Constabulary who oversees the work of regional offices. Some Inspectors have a very specific function—such as training.

NCIS National Criminal Intelligence Service. Set up to develop intelligence on high-level criminals. Now absorbed into SOCPA.

NCPE National Centre for Policing Excellence.

NCS National Crime Squad. Organisation responsible for investigating major crime on a national basis. Now absorbed into SOCPA.

NPIA National Police Improvement Agency.

PITO Police Information Technology Organisation (now absorbed into NPIA).

Police Federation Like the police officers' trade union (at least for officers of the ranks from constable up to chief inspector). Set up under an Act of Parliament, the Federation has regional offices across England and Wales and a national office in Surrey. Each force has a number of Federation representatives who are elected by its members. They will provide advice on aspects of welfare, conditions of service, discipline and health and safety.

PSU Police Standards Unit. This Unit provides guidance at a strategic level to police forces on maintaining standards.

Superintendents' Association Similar to the Federation but for Superintendents and Chief Superintendents.

Common abbreviations and jargon

ABH Actual bodily harm—an offence under section 47 of the Offences Against the Person Act 1861. Generally involves a fairly high degree of injury like lost tooth and bad bruising. See also section 47 and OAP.

ACC Assistant Chief Constable.

ACR Area control room.

AFIS Automated fingerprint identification system.

Airwave Digital radio system used by all officers and forces.

ANPR Automated Number Plate Recognition system.

Appropriate adult Every person under 17 who is in custody and being interviewed requires the assistance of an appropriate adult. Usually a parent or guardian but not necessarily. Also required by other vulnerable people in custody such as people with mental difficulties.

APS Acting police sergeant. Applies to other ranks as well, e.g. A/CI = acting chief inspector.

ARV Armed response vehicle.

ASBO Anti-social behaviour order. Order passed by the courts to stop people whose behaviour is making their neighbours' lives miserable. The police and local authority can apply for them.

BCU Basic command unit.

Brief A lawyer representing defendant. Occasionally used to describe a warrant card.

C & D Complaints and discipline department. Now more usually known as Professional Standards Department or PSD (see below).

CDRP Crime and Disorder Reduction Partnership—set up under the Crime and Disorder Act 1998.

CHIS Covert human intelligence source (informant).

CIS Crime information/intelligence system.

CJSU Criminal justice support unit. Department responsible for managing proposed prosecution files and related matters. See also CJU.

CJU Criminal justice unit—same as CJSU.

Club number See CRO number.

Con & Use The Road Vehicles (Construction and Use) Regulations. Amended frequently and containing masses of useful detail about vehicles such as how much tread they have to have on their tyres and what sort of condition they have to be in, and less useful bits such as the requirements of motorised hedge trimmers and whether trailers carrying timber are exempt from having mud-flaps.

CRO number Criminal Records Office number. Every convicted person is allocated one of these. Recorded on PNC. See also Club number.

D & C Discipline and complaints department—now more usually known as Professional Standards Department or PSD (see below).

D & D Drunk and disorderly. The offence committed where someone is disorderly while drunk in a public place.

Dep/DCC Deputy Chief Constable.

DNA Deoxyribonucleic acid (see why it's just called DNA?). Gene identification. Found in hair, semen and other samples that are taken from suspects or recovered from crime scenes.

DPA Data Protection Act.

DSU Divisional support unit.

Due care Driving without due care and attention. Probably the most common motoring offence. Includes everything from ignoring road signs to driving through puddles and splashing pedestrians.

Egress Normally used in crime reports to refer to the way a criminal got out of a building. Egress is the opposite of 'entry' and often criminals use a different way out from the way they got in.

FPN Fixed Penalty Notice.

FPND Fixed Penalty Notice for Disorder—may be issued for certain offences such as section 5 (see below).

HORT/1 Home Office Road Traffic 1 form—also known as a producer, this is the piece of paper that officers give to motorists allowing them seven days to produce their driving documents at a police station of their choice.

IO Investigation officer.

IP Injured party or person (victim).

MFH Missing from home.

MO Modus operandi. The method of operating used by a particular criminal (e.g. always wears a mask, kicks in kitchen door).

MOP Member of the public.

MSU Mobile support unit.

NFA 'No further action' (method of writing off police calls or tasks) or 'no fixed abode'.

NIM National Intelligence Model.

NIP Notice of Intended Prosecution. Notice (oral or in writing) that you have to give motorists within 14 days before reporting them for certain road traffic offences (such as speeding) unless they have had an accident at the time.

OAP Offences Against the Person Act 1861.

OPL Over the prescribed limit (driving whilst...). See also Poz alco.

PI Participating informant—person (non-police) who has been authorised to play a limited part in criminal activity in order to catch offenders.

PII Public interest immunity—legal expression whereby the police and others apply to a court to prevent documents or other evidence from being used, usually because it would pose a threat to public interest (e.g. because an informant is named in the document).

PNC Police National Computer. Contains details of all people with criminal convictions, etc. See also CRO number.

Poz alco Positive alcohol—driving while over the prescribed alcohol limit. See also OPL.

PSD Professional Standards Department—the people who deal with discipline and complaints against police officers.

PSU Police support unit.

Reg 9 Form that is served on police officers (under Regulation 9 of the Police (Conduct) Regulations 1999) warning them that they are being investigated for possible criminal/conduct offences.

Section 4 Offence of putting person in fear of unlawful violence (Public Order Act 1986).

Section 5 Offence of using threatening, abusive or insulting words or behaviour (Public Order Act 1986).

Section 29 production Power to allow prisoners out of custody so that they can help the police with enquiries into other offences. Taken from section 29 of the Criminal Justice Act 1961.

Section 47 See also ABH and OAP.

Section 136 The power to remove people from public places if they appear to be suffering from a mental disorder. Taken from the Mental Health Act 1983.

SIO Senior investigating officer.

Skipper Sergeant (usually heard in South East England).

SOCO Scenes of crime officer.

Super Superintendent (now seldom used).

TDA Offence of 'taking and driving away' (Theft Act 1968, section 12). Referred to in newspapers as 'joy riding'. See also UTMV, TWOC and TWLA.

TWLA Offence of 'taking without lawful authority' (Theft Act 1968, section 12).

TWOC Offence of taking conveyance without the owner's consent (Theft Act 1968, section 12).

UTMV Offence of unlawful taking of motor vehicle (Theft Act 1968, section 12).

Appendix 2

THE PHONETIC ALPHABET

A great deal of police communication is done via the radio network. The network is now digital and gives a much higher quality of reception than anything the police have experienced before. Despite the high quality it is essential that when passing a message an officer does so as accurately as possible, and the area that has the greatest capacity for mistakes is when giving a name, address or vehicle registration number. For this reason the police use the standard phonetic alphabet in which each letter has an associated word. If you do join the police service you will need to know this alphabet, and it is worth learning it sooner rather than later (not only that, but it does crop up in the occasional pub quiz).

The standard alphabet used by the UK police, emergency services and armed forces is as follows:

A	Alpha	H	Hotel	O	Oscar	U	Uniform
B	Bravo	I	India	P	Papa	V	Victor
C	Charlie	J	Juliet	Q	Quebec	W	Whiskey
D	Delta	K	Kilo	R	Romeo	X	X-ray
E	Echo	L	Lima	S	Sierra	Y	Yankee
F	Foxtrot	M	Mike	T	Tango	Z	Zulu
G	Golf	N	November				

The Irish spelling of 'Whiskey' is deliberate, but not compulsory.

Bibliography

Websites

There seem to be hundreds if not thousands of websites relating to the police and policing in England and Wales. Sometimes the easiest thing to do is put what you are looking for into your favourite search engine and click the button. However, the list below may save you some time—these are websites that have been referred to in the text or which may be of use to you if you want to know more about the subjects we have covered. For ease of use they have been broken down into categories with an explanatory note for each.

Recruiting and training

<http://www.policecouldyou.co.uk>
A Government-owned website solely about police recruitment. This site contains a lot of useful information to the potential recruit and you can download an application form.

<http://www.policeuk.com/>
This is not an official site but it does have a lot of useful information. In particular it has a well run and well used forum in which applicants and student officers openly share their experiences and knowledge.

<http://www.skillsforjustice.com/>
If you want to find out details of the 22 National Occupational Standards that apply to student officers this is the place to come.

<http://www.reviewing.co.uk/research/experiential.learning. htm>
This is a very good site in which the theories underpinning experiential learning are explored in layman's terms.

The history and development of policing

The law school at Leeds University has made available two series of notes on the history and development of policing in England and Wales. They are both very interesting reads and will give you a good insight into the subjects covered. They can be found at:

<http://www.leeds.ac.uk/law/staff/lawdw/cyberpolice/pol1.htm>
This one deals with the historical development of policing.

<http://www.leeds.ac.uk/law/teaching/law6cw/police/pol-ho1. htm>
This one looks at the relationship between the Home Office and the police. It's a fascinating read and offers a view on this very important subject not commonly aired in policing circles.

Law and legal knowledge

<http://www.blackstonespolicemanuals.com>
Blackstone's are the main publishers of the standard police text books.

<http://www.opsi.gov.uk>
The Office of Public Sector Information is a site well worth becoming familiar with. Using its search function will give you access to all sorts of useful information, including all the Acts of Parliament.

General police interest

<http://www.homeoffice.gov.uk>
The official Home Office website. Through it you can access the official view on just about any subject to do with policing. The section on police reform is particularly useful and interesting if you want to know where Her Majesty's Government intends to take the police service in the medium to long term.

<http://www.inspectorates.homeoffice.gov.uk/hmic>
This the site of Her Majesty's Inspectorate of Constabulary; another useful place to find out about future developments and the source of many reports which are driving the Service today, notably Training Matters.

<http://info.policereview.com/>
Police Review is the 'trade paper' of the Service. It is published weekly by Jane's and always has lots of articles of interest to the serving officer.

<http://www.polfed.org/>
The Police Federation is the 'trade union' of officers up to and including chief inspector level; so, as you would expect, their site is well worth keeping an eye on.

<http://www.criminal-courts-review.org.uk>
On this site you will find the review of the criminal courts carried out in 2001. It's a fascinating read not least because it gives a view of the workings of the courts from 'the other side'. It is also kept reasonably up to date with information about the ongoing reform of the court system.

<http://www.archive.official-documents.co.uk/document/cm42/ 4262/4262.htm>
Here you will find the full text of the Macpherson Report, the finding of the enquiry into the police actions connected with the murder of Stephen Lawrence. This report has had a massive impact on how the police carry out their duties, yet it is one of the misquoted and misunderstood documents of recent history. If you are serious about a career in the police you should take time to read this report in full.

Books

There are almost as many books about policing as there are websites. Below is a list that may be of interest in further reading after you have read this book. The list is by no means exhaustive; in particular you may want to look at the Oxford University Press catalogue of police-related books (available through the Blackstone's website given above). As you can find a synopsis on-line of just about every book, no notes are included for those mentioned here—they are, however, broken down into the same categories as above.

Recruiting and training

J. Moon, *A Handbook of Reflective and Experiential Learning: Theory and Practice*, 2004, Routledge Falmer

S. Sutcliffe & W. Francis, *Passing the Police Recruit Assessment Process*, 2007, Law Matters Publishing

H. Tolley, C. Tolley, B. Hodge, *How to Pass the New Police Selection System*, 2004, Kogan Page

C.J. Tyreman, *Police Initial Recruitment Test (Mock Test With Preparation)*, 2003, ELC Publications

The history and development of policing

C. Emsley, *The English Police: A Political and Social History*, 1996, Longman

C. Emsley, *Crime and Society in England, 1750–1900*, 2004, Longman

N. Walker, *Policing in a Changing Constitutional Order*, 2000, Sweet and Maxwell

Law and legal knowledge

C. Allen, *Practical Guide to Evidence*, 2004, Cavendish Publishing Ltd

Brian Fitzpatrick, *Going to Court*, 2006, Oxford University Press

R. Huxley-Binns, *Unlocking the English Legal System*, 2005, Hodder Arnold

General police interest

P.B. Ainsworth, *Psychology and Policing*, 2002, Willan Publishing

D. Copperfield, *Wasting Police Time: The Crazy World of the War on Crime*, 2006, Monday Books

Home Office research study No 249, *The Economic and Social Costs of Class A Drug Use in England and Wales*, 2000

Sir Robert Mark, *In the Office of Constable*, 1978, HarperCollins

Index